Fishing For Smallmouth Bass

Mike Mladenik

Contents

Introduction

In my youth, most of my time on the water was spent fishing for largemouth bass and panfish, not that there is anything wrong with that! Those early efforts left me with many fond memories and a boat full of knowledge. This interest in fishing helped me to figure out at an early age that living in the Chicago suburbs was no place for an aspiring fisherman.

In the early 1970's I bought a piece of land in Crivitz, Wisconsin. I would head up north on weekends with my only concern being the decision regarding what water to fish and what species to pursue. Through these weekend adventures on the water I quickly developed a fondness for smallmouth bass. Up north I was in my element and had the option of fishing in a variety of natural lakes, reservoirs and rivers. It was tough fishing only on weekends since my construction job did not allow for summer vacations. Eventually, I made the move and parted ways with the big city.

By 1980 my guiding career was in full swing. Guiding in northern Wisconsin meant fishing primarily for walleye and musky so I followed suit, putting smallmouth bass on the back burner. However, while guiding for walleyes I would accidentally stumble on a bunch of scrappy smallmouth. Gradually, these "chance" encounters with smallmouth bass became more common and most of my clients figured out that these meetings were not accidental.

Smallmouth bass became my passion. I was blessed to spend most of my life fishing for smallmouth bass on the rivers, lakes and reservoirs of northern Wisconsin and Michigan's Upper Peninsula. I could fish a deep clear natural lake one day, a stained water reservoir the next and head for the river during the Dog Days of Summer. The diversity in the type of water allowed me to perfect a variety of presentations to put my clients on smallmouth regardless of the conditions.

It's no secret that if given the option I would prefer to catch a smallmouth on a topwater lure even if it means reducing my success rate. The key to a successful day on the water is in knowing both where to fish and choosing the proper presentation. Knowing when to keep the topwater bait in the tackle box and drag a tube or cast a jerkbait will yield a great day on the water. Many of my clients have the same passion for smallmouth bass and I try to share my experience with them so they can become a better smallmouth angler and make the right choices.

Over the last 40 years, 30 of which have been spent as a full time fishing guide, I focused as much of my efforts as was possible hunting for big smallmouth bass. During that time I have logged in thousands of hours, catching in excess of 60,000 smallmouth. Over a thousand of these smallmouth measured on the plus size of 20 inches, with six pound fish being caught every year. While I've successfully landed a handful of toads that hit the scale at 7 pounds, an eight pounder is at the top of my bucket list. If and when I ever retire from guiding this could become a full time job, wherever it leads me.

A fishing guide has to be versatile and accommodate the needs of his clients even if they have irrational and unrealistic expectations. There have been days that while jigging for walleyes under a tough bite I have had to painfully observe big smallmouth schooling baitfish or feeding on an insect hatch. We could have had a field day catching smallmouth but bagged only a few legal walleyes. That makes for a painstakingly long day for a smallmouth bass aficionado. Simply put, I only fish for other types of fish when I am getting paid!

Chapter 1
Getting Started

The first tool to consider when hitting the water is your choice of fishing rod. Fishing rods come in all lengths, quality levels and prices. In the past, anglers had limited choices both in rod material and rod style, with most people just looking at the price. Today, fishing rods range in price from $25 to $400 and while price is still often the deciding factor on the type of rod an angler may purchase, today's anglers have a much greater selection. However, when buying a rod, keep in mind that you get what you pay for. A good quality rod will last a lifetime and if it does break, most reputable manufacturers have some sort of warranty.

Years back when I started guiding I had only one or two quality fishing rods. One time in early spring, I was showing my client my new high-end fishing rod. His response was, "You don't need an expensive rod to catch fish, I've been using this rod for years and have caught tons of fish." The old timer's rod looked as old as he was and the rod guides were held on with duct tape. On that particular day my client had a point. The smallmouth were hitting leeches as fast as they hit the water. There was no need for casting distance or accuracy let alone a sensitive fishing rod. A kid with a $10 rod and reel combo could have caught as many fish as a pro.

Fishing For Smallmouth Bass

Those days are now few and far between and for every day like that, there are dozens of days when the angler who had the right rod for the situation caught the most fish. Everyone knows that you can't use your ultra-light panfish rod to catch muskies, but when bass fishing you can't use the same rod when casting soft plastics and deep diving crankbaits. You don't need to have 20 rods in the boat but your success rate will improve if you have the right tool for the job. On the other end of the spectrum, a top of the line fishing rod probably won't help a beginning angler. You need to find the right balance to match your angling ability and pocketbook.

The average angler will walk into a bait shop or big box store with good intentions to purchase a new fishing rod. He or she will pick up a rod from the rack and start shaking it vigorously. They usually put the rod back in the rack, grab another one and repeat the procedure several times. Eventually they will be down to two rods, put one in each hand, shake them and choose the one that they think feels right.

There is nothing wrong with choosing a rod that feels right, but is it the right tool for the job? There is a reason that rod manufacturers put ratings on the rod just before the handle which rates the rods' action and preferred line weight. There is consistent scientific methodology that all rod manufacturers use to rate their rods, and, for the most part, if anglers pay attention to the rod rating they can't go wrong.

The most critical factor when choosing a rod is the rods' action. Action is a measurement of deflection or flex that the rod exhibits under load, and more importantly, where that flex occurs along the rod blank. "Extra Fast" action rods flex more towards the tip. "Slow" action rods distribute the flex progressively throughout the entire rod blank.

The next thing to consider is the rods' power. Power is defined by the amount of pressure required to flex the rod blank. Most rods are designed to optimally manage a specific range of lure and line weights. The heavier the line and lure, the more power you'll need to cast, fight and pull effectively. The lighter the line and lure, the less power you will need.

The measurement of the change in the diameter of the rod blank from the tip to the butt is known as the taper. Many use the term synonymously with the rods' action. An aggressive taper at the tip creates a faster action. A straight taper (one which changes at an equal rate throughout the rod blank) creates a moderate or slower action.

At one time fiberglass was the main rod component but today's rods are constructed of composite graphite. Composite graphite rods are made with a blend of high-modulus graphite fibers and are the backbone of the industry. The higher the tensile strength of the fiber the stronger, more sensitive the rod will be. This is also indicative of a high quality rod. High quality rods require more man hours in their construction which contributes to their higher price. Fishing rod technology is increasing the strength and sensitivity of the modern fishing rod.

Fiberglass rods remain in production but are used for specific applications. One example would be when fishing a crankbait when the slower response of the fiberglass will allow for a better hookset. With a high-modulus graphite rod the angler can respond to the strike too quickly and set the hook before the fish has the crankbait. Anglers who troll also prefer fiberglass rods since they will absorb some of the shock when the fish hits the bait.

Over the years I have worked with a few rod manufacturers who make top quality rods. Many of these rods worked fine for most applications but they needed a bit of tweaking. Since the perfect rod was not available, the next step was to design rods made to my specifications. With the help of my good friend Jim Grandt (who has been making quality fishing rods for 30 years) and intense field testing, I developed Smallmouth Plus Series rods.

Smallmouth Plus Series rods have blank through touch reel seat handle construction which gives them performance beyond the competition. Sleek, low frame design combines maximum sensitivity along with total control when fighting a monster smallmouth. All Smallmouth Plus Series rods are constructed using a 58 million modulus high strain graphite blank, the industry's leading technology.

Smallmouth Rod Recommendation

lure	line	action	power	length
jigs/live bait	4-6	fast	light	6'6"- 7'
plastics	4-8	fast	medium -medium light	6'6"- 7'
topwater	6-10	moderate	medium	6'6"- 7'
crankbaits	8-10	moderate	medium	6'6"- 7'
spinnerbaits	8-12	moderate	medium - medium heavy	6'6"

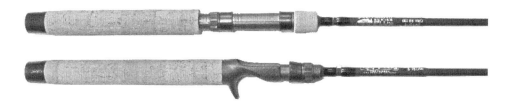

The spinning rods have a short fore-cork so you can put your finger on the blank for even more sensitivity. The 13 inch handle adds three inches to the rod length from the end of the fore-grip allowing for maximum balance when combined with a quality lightweight reel. Durable construction utilizing Nitride plated stainless ultra-thin rings set into marine grade stainless frames virtually eliminates cracks or ring failure, creates less drag on the ring, insures unmatched ring performance and produces great results with braided lines.

Reels

The choice in spinning or bait casting reel will first off depend on the lures and line being used. In general, spinning reels are preferred for casting light lines and smaller lures, while casting rods are preferred for heavy baits and large lures. Spin cast reels, referred to as closed faced spinning reels, are still used by some anglers but are high maintenance. As a guide, I go into panic mode anytime I see a client bring a spin cast reel into the boat. I detest spin casting reels so much that I will not set aside any space in this book for them.

The gear ratio of the reel is critical for proper lure retrieve, yet few anglers pay any attention to the gear ratio when purchasing a reel. The higher the gear ratio the reel has the more line that is retrieved with each crank of the reel. A reel with a gear ratio of 5.0:1 will retrieve 20-24" with each crank of the reel, a 6.0:1 will retrieve 26-28" and a 7.0:1 will retrieve 28"-31." Both spinning and casting reels come in the various gear ratios needed to run lures effectively.

In recent years casting reels have been greatly improved and they contain anti-backlash magnets. Anglers no longer need to master the fine art of "thumbing" the spool on the cast to prevent line overrun. If the brakes are adjusted properly overrun is greatly reduced. The better the quality (and price) of the bait caster the easier it is to adjust the brakes. If the brakes are adjusted properly overrun is greatly reduced, or with some reels, virtually eliminated.

When casting crankbaits and spinnerbaits, low gear ratio bait casters are preferred by most anglers. Besides allowing the crankbait or spinnerbait to run at the desired depth and speed the slower gear ratio is easier on the angler. If an angler used a large spool capacity spinning reel he would be putting wasted stress on his arm and hand and still not be working the bait properly. One thing I have learned over the years is not to make fishing any harder than need be.

Some anglers will use bait casters with a 6.0:1 for plastic worms and it works fine. Personally, I prefer a medium sized spinning reel with six or eight pound test. Most medium sized spinning reels have the right gear ratio to work most soft plastics. Spinning reels are more forgiving when fishing tight to or under cover. With a bait caster, one slip and you have an overrun. Spinning rods are also far superior when working light jigs or live bait rigs.

Another thing to consider when purchasing a fishing reel is the bearings. The number of ball bearings determines the smoothness of the reel. Spinning and bait casting reels all feature either ball bearings or bushings strategically placed within the reel for smoothness, support and stability. Many spinning reels also feature a roller bearing within the line roller. When it comes to smooth performance and durability, sealed stainless steel ball bearings are preferable over bushings. Generally speaking, the more ball bearings a reel has, the more smoothly it will perform. Quality reels typically feature at least two stainless steel ball bearings. Top-of-the-line models usually boast about four to six ball bearings; however, some of the newer deluxe spinning reels on the market feature up to 12.

Drag is something you'll need to understand and know how to use if you plan on being a successful angler. The object of drag is to allow the spool to slip before the line snaps. This slipping of the spool allows the fish more line and also prevents it from breaking. When fighting a fish, the rod does its job by absorbing the shock from the line. The rod and the drag work together to prevent the line from stretching and possibly breaking while fighting the fish.

You may be wondering, "If setting the drag tires out the fish, why not just tighten it down all the way to begin with?" There are a couple of reasons why you don't want to do this: first of all, it will increase the tension on the line, possibly causing it to break. Secondly, adding too much pressure could cause the lure to be ripped from the fish's mouth during the fight. Either way the fish is getting away from you.

Adjusting the drag is done in various ways depending on manufacturer and model. You'll want to look at the instructions with your reel to determine how to operate the drag. Listed below are some of the more common ways to adjust the drag.

1) A number system 1-10
2) An arrow pointing to the words **less** or **more**
3) Located near the handle *(called a star drag)*.

Take some time and learn how to adjust the drag for your reel. Adjusting it will either make the fish fight harder or it will make it easier on him to pull line from the spool. I suggest playing with this setting so you'll get comfortable making the proper adjustment when the time comes. Keep in mind; it's something that may need to be changed several times a day depending on how the fish are fighting.

Remember, too much tension and pressure on the line might break the line or cause the lure to be ripped from the fish's mouth during the fight. On the flip side, if the drag is set too loose the fish will run, potentially taking your line around stumps and rocks etc. until it breaks. The fish could also simply shake his head, and, because of the slack on the line, the lure comes free.

The composition and design of the spool should be a consideration when purchasing either a spinning or bait casting reel. Spinning reels typically come with either an anodized aluminum spool or a graphite spool. The anodized aluminum spool offers greater strength and durability than graphite spools, which can break or crack under torque. As far as spinning reel spool design is concerned, there are two basic types – internal spool and skirted spool varieties. While some anglers swear by the performance and simplicity of the older-style internal spool models, more advanced spinning reels typically feature skirted spools. The "skirt" helps prevent line from becoming entangled within the housing of the reel. Additional skirted spinning reel spool options include the choice of a standard spool, or a shallower, elongated "long cast" spool design. In theory, the newer long-cast spool design allows for reduced line friction, resulting in greater casting distance.

Most bait casting reels feature machined, anodized aluminum spools, however, some models may feature spools composed of graphite. Again, the anodized aluminum spools provide greater strength and long-lasting performance. For even greater durability, anglers can opt for a conventional reel with a chromed, bronze or stainless steel spool. While these spools do not spin as freely as those made of anodized aluminum or graphite, they offer the highest level of strength and corrosion resistance. Metal spools like these are best for heavy-duty angling applications, or when specialty lines like Dacron or Wire are being used.

Line memory can be a problem with spinning reels. If a spinning reel is not used for a while the memory will cause the line to come off the spool in a coil. When line reaches this point the angler has two options. He can either respool with fresh line, or stretch out the line. The best way to stretch the line is to pull off much of the spool, tie on a weight and pull the line behind the boat for a few minutes.

There are many different types of fishing line available to the angler and choosing the right line can be confusing. Unfortunately, there is no one fishing line that is perfect for all situations. You can ask five different anglers what the best line for a specific presentation is and you might get five different answers. Choosing the right line is thus often simply a matter of personal choice. However, if you weigh the advantages and disadvantages to each type of line you can make the choice easier.

Before the discovery of nylon, braided Dacron was the most popular line. However, Dacron possessed poor knot strength, low abrasion resistance and little stretch so it was used much less after monofilament line was introduced. Today, Dacron maintains only a very small niche in the marketplace, especially with the introduction of super braided lines. It is used primarily for trolling and by old school musky fisherman since it should only be used with casasting reels.

In 1938, DuPont announced the discovery of nylon, a "group of new synthetic super polymers" that could be made into textile fibers stronger and more elastic than cotton, silk, wool, or rayon. The next year, DuPont began commercial production of nylon monofilamentfishing line. This new line, primitive by today's standards, didn't catch on immediately; older fishing lines, particularly braided Dacron, remained popular for the next two decades.

Monofilament line remains popular, accounting for more than two-thirds of all fishing lines sold. Monofilament line is formed through an extrusion process in which molten plastic is formed into a strand through a die. This process is relatively inexpensive, producing a less costly product which adds to the popularity of monofilament line.

Monofilament is a better choice than braided line for the average angler but you will have to deal with the line stretch and memory. Memory causes coils in the line that can make a soft bite tough to detect. One way to avoid the memory of monofilament line is to change your line before your first fishing trip of the year. Don't carry a filler spool loaded with line. When line is on a filler spool it will develop more memory than when it is in use. Too much stretch in your line will make hookset difficult. If you don't want to buy a bulk spool of line, stop at a bait shop and have them spool up your reel with fresh line. While monofilament line might not be the best choice for every situation it is workable in just about any situation.

In the early 1990s, gel-spun and aramid fibers such as Spectra, Kevlar and Dyneema entered the fishing line market, creating a new category of braided lines often called "superlines." These synthetic fibers are thin and incredibly strong (more than 10 times stronger than steel). Individual fiber strands are joined through an intricate, time-consuming braiding process to produce ultrathin, super strong, sensitive, yet expensive lines.

Anglers who experimented with early superlines were frustrated by low knot strength, backlashes, poor coloration, damaged equipment, impossible snags, and more. To many, these disadvantages outweighed the benefits of strength, micro diameter, and ultra-sensitivity. However, makers of superlines have made continual advances and improvements to the raw material fibers and the process that converts them into fishing line. Coloration, castability and strength have all been improved, overcoming some early disadvantages.

Because of its smaller diameter anglers can spool more line on their reels. Superlines have little stretch, transmitting strikes instantly to the rod tip. However, this extra sensitivity can cause anglers to set the hook too quickly. In cold water, the bite can be light and reacting too fast to the pick-up will result in missed fish. Braided line will also sink slower and under windy conditions will not allow the bait to fall to the desired depth.

Superlines require a Palomar knot for best results. Put mono backing on your reel before spooling superlines to prevent "slipping" on the reel and to conserve line. This also adds firmness to the spool for better casting and less backlashes. Tie a Uni knot to connect to the mono. Do not overfill reels with superline. Overfilling creates loose strands after a cast and more backlashes. Fill to one-eighth inch from the spool rim.

Fluorocarbon line is a polymer that's nearly invisible in water and it doesn't absorb water. Fluorocarbon fishing leaders originated in Japan, where anglers are particularly fussy about bait presentations. Japanese fisheries are heavily pressured, so lifelike bait presentations are important. Nearly invisible fluorocarbon lines enhanced this quality.

American anglers began using fluorocarbon leaders, primarily in saltwater and fly fishing applications, for the same reason the Japanese were using it -- low visibility. It caught on when anglers reported catching more fish with it. The original fluorocarbon leaders were stiff and very expensive, but new technologies have produced more flexible fluorocarbon at more affordable prices.

Fluorocarbon certainly offers advantages in clear-water situations where fish are heavily pressured or slow to bite. Also, because fluorocarbon does not absorb water, it won't weaken or increase in stretch like nylon fishing line. Added density makes fluorocarbon very abrasion-resistant, so it's ideal for rough conditions, and makes it sink faster than nylon lines, so lures dive deeper and faster. And because fluorocarbon stretches more slowly and far less than nylon, particularly when compared to wet nylon, it's much more sensitive.

Fluorocarbon lines, like superlines, require special attention. The

Fishing For Smallmouth Bass

Palomar knot is the best to use with this type of line. Fluorocarbons are still stiffer than nylon, even when wet. This requires more attentiveness to the line when casting, and finer "balance" of tackle. If heavier fluorocarbon line is used on lighter rods, reels and lures, anglers will experience more difficulty. Bait casting reels may require additional adjustment for the extra momentum created by the heavier weight of fluorocarbon. Adjust mechanical brakes to the weight of the line and lure to maximize casting distance and minimize overruns.

Hybrid lines are a blend of nylon and fluorocarbon and are specifically made for spinning tackle because of its low memory features that are crucial for spinning gear. Besides being significantly more supple, hybrid line is still abrasion resistant; it is also water proof, UV resistant, and has less stretch than monofilaments. The high density of fluorocarbon creates increased strength as well.

Grubs

A grub is nothing more than a long slender chunk of plastic with a curly or straight tail, or as many anglers refer to them, "a jig and twister tail". The Mister Twister Curly Tail grub was created in a small town when a fisherman using a pressure cooker melted down old plastic and melted it into book molds. Prior to the development of the curly tail grub in 1972 plastic lures were worms or grubs with little or no action and they were hard to the touch. Although curly tail grubs have been around for a long time they will still catch bass consistently.

However, in recent years due to all the new innovations in plastics they have taken a back seat and many younger bassers don't even know they exist. At times, grubs are the only thing that works and there have been many days on the water when if I would have switched to grubs earlier in the day, my success rate would have been much higher.

Although grubs will catch bass spring, summer and fall, many anglers fail to understand their versatility and how to use them effectively. It is common for anglers to take a grub out of their tackle box, rig it on any old jighead or hook and just start casting. Sure, on occasion they'll catch a bass, but most of the time they will get the grub hung up on a rock or tree, break it off and tie on a different bait. Many of todays anglers just don't have the patience to master the fine art of fishing with grubs.

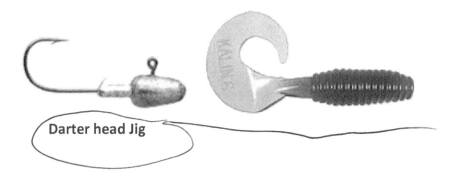

Darter head Jig

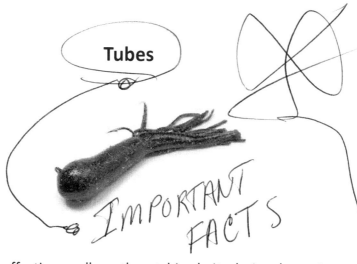

Tubes

IMPORTANT FACTS

Tubes are effective smallmouth catching baits during the entire open water period. Tubes can be fished around all types of cover due to their unlimited rigging options. They are one of the only baits that I have enabled me to catch bass regardless of the weather pattern. Form stable weather patterns to the most adverse cold front, if you can't hook a bass on a tube I doubt any other bait will work.

Being a smallmouth aficionado, most of my experience with tubes has been in pursuit of these denizens. Most of the time, I will use a 3-inch or smaller tube on light or medium light action spinning tackle. When rigging a tube for smallmouth I find myself using the basic method of inserting a jighead into the hollow body of the tube. This finesse presentation will work both on clear water natural lakes and stained water reservoirs and rivers.

Rigging a tube with a jighead will allow the angler to catch smallmouth regardless of their mood. However, the action of the tube can be affected by the position of the jig head inside the tube body. With the head pushed all the way forward, tubes tend to fall faster with less spiral, which is great for active smallmouth. When smallmouth are less-aggressive, slow down the fall of the tube and increase the spiral, by positioning the jig head back from the nose of the tube. Changing the way the tube is rigged on the same jighead can turn a slow day into a banner outing. There have been many occasions when what seemed like a slight modification resulted in a change in the bite. On a few rare occasions a radical change yielded outstanding results.

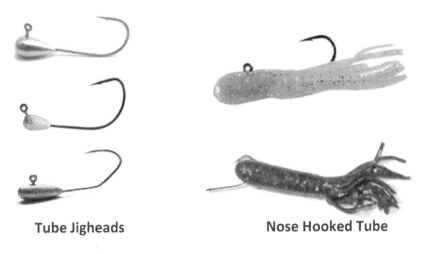

Tube Jigheads   **Nose Hooked Tube**

TRY THESE

Skirted Grubs

Skirted grubs are also called Hula grubs or spider jigs and are made by a host of manufacturers. Three and four inch skirted grubs are the most popular with anglers. They come in both single-tail and twin-tail configurations. The skirt on the front of the grub body slows the jig's rate of fall and pulses enticingly in the water. The curly tail undulates when you pull it through the water. Most skirted grubs are impregnated with salt and are scented with garlic.

Finesse Worms

Finesse worms. These plastic worms are thin, short worms of 3 to 4 inches (7.5 to 10 cm), designed to fish with light tackle in clear water conditions, such as those found in older reservoirs that have lost most of their grass and sunken timber cover. They are often fished with light split shot or "Slider" jig heads.

Straight-tail worms. These worms, usually 6 inches (15 cm) in length, resemble nightcrawlers in appearance, usually in everything but color. These worms are usually retrieved straight, although they can also be fished in a "lift-and-drop" style.

(Stick Baits)

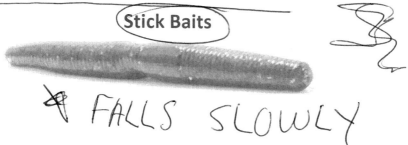

This was the bait that I was looking for, but little did I know that it would change the way I fish and be a Godsend for me and countless fishing guides across the country. The stick bait falls slowly through the water column and is irresistible for finicky smallmouth bass.

I have been on a mission to perfect using stick baits for river and reservoir smallmouth and have caught thousands of smallmouth. It is easy to use and works under most conditions making it the ideal method for a guide.

Soft Plastic Jerkbaits

Minnow style jerkbaits are effective in all types of cover but shine when fished around wood cover and weeds. While soft plastic jerkbaits remain effective when smallmouth are relating to wood cover it is an essential part of my arsenal when fishing mid-river weeds. I use both floating and sinking jerkbaits when fishing river grass depending on both the current and density of the grass. If the grass is thick, I will use an unweighted jerkbait rigged on a wide gap hook and let the bait drift over the grass.

Patience is a virtue when fishing jerkbaits. An aggressive twitch of the rod might trigger an active smallmouth but it won't entice a neutral or inactive one. Many of the largest smallmouth I catch are taken by finessing the jerkbait. I will let the jerkbait sink, and with slack line I raise my rod about one foot and let it drop. I watch my line for any movement signaling that a bass has grabbed my jerkbait. When I see a smallmouth pick up the jerkbait, I slowly reel in the slack and set the hook when I feel the slightest pressure.

Crankbaits

Crankbaits will catch smallmouth bass in all types of water. The critical factor is using the right crankbait for the depth of water that you are fishing. Lipless crankbaits are excellent in clear water but in stained water I have had a higher success rate with lipped crankbaits. Lipped crankbaits will have a wider action that is more desirable in stained water. Color is also important and the rule of thumb is the darker the water the brighter the color. In clear water top colors are blue, black/silver and shad colors work best and in stained water try red, fire tiger and perch.

When fishing deep diving crankbaits it is important to use long rods which will allow the angler to make longer casts. It takes a crankbait about one third of the casting distance to reach its maximum depth penetration. So if you make a 30 yard cast, you have 30 feet of maximum depth presentation. Fluorocarbon line will also help the crankbait reach maximum depth penetration as well.

Hard Jerkbaits

Suspending jerkbaits, which are crankbaits that are designed to be stopped and left suspending, will catch big bass but they are not for everyone. Most anglers fish suspending jerkbaits too quickly and defeat the purpose of the bait. I will cast out the bait, let it sit for about 10 seconds and give it a short twitch. I will again let the jerkbait drop and suspend for a long as 30 seconds. This retrieve will catch big bass but most anglers are short on patience.

Topwater

Poppers

Poppers attract bass with a gurgling and popping sound on the water's surface. Poppers should be retrieved in a series of starts and stops. Cast the lure out and let it rest a few minutes. Then retrieve it a few feet and let it rest again. The popping and gurgling will gain the fish's attention. The strike usually occurs when the lure is at rest. Fish them around weedlines, stumps, and shorelines. Experiment with retrieves as bass will want it fast one day, and very slow the next.

Prop Baits

Prop baits create a disturbance when jerked slightly. They work best when the water temperature is above 60 degrees. Work close to cover on heavy tackle or off long points on drop-offs on lighter tackle. Examples of propbaits are the Hubs Chub, Devils Horse, and Torpedo baits. Tie directly to the bait and let it sit for a while after casting it out before starting a twitching retrieve back to the boat. In calm water use a slow, quiet retrieve. In choppy water use a noisy retrieve.

Stick Baits

Stick baits have no action of their own and require the fisherman's skill to make them perform maneuvers such as "walking the dog." These baits work well in open water, and around boat docks, tree lines, stump rows, etc. The most popular stick bait is the Zara Spook, and for good reasons. This bait has been catching largemouth and smallmouth alike for decades, often two at a time! It calls in fish from as deep as 25 feet and works under a variety of conditions. It works best during the summer and can be fished all day. The most productive colors all have one thing in common: a white belly. Tie the lure on using a large snap.

The most popular retrieve is 'walking the dog'. It takes some practice to achieve the proper jerk, pause, jerk cadence to walk the dog. It helps to have someone who has mastered the technique show you. You may have to keep the rod tip up the first 10 feet or so on long casts, then lower the tip and work it back in. If a fish misses it, keep going with the cadence - they'll come back and hit it again.

Buzzbaits

Buzzbaits are similar to spinnerbaits but are designed to be fished on top. Fish them right across logjams, submerged weeds, sparse grass, etc. Buzzbaits produce best from mid-spring to mid-fall when water temperature is above 65 degrees. They can be fished in, around, through and over cover due to its shape and design. They also produce best with a slow, erratic presentation.

Rods

The first tool to consider when hitting the water is your choice of fishing rod. Fishing rods come in all lengths and prices. In the past, anglers had limited choices both in rod material and rod style, with most people just looking at the price. Today, fishing rods range in price from $50 to $400 and while price is still often the deciding factor on their purchase is should not be the main factor. However, when buying a rod, keep in mind that you get what you pay for. A good quality rod will last a lifetime and if it does break, most reputable manufacturers have some sort of warranty.

The most critical factor when choosing a rod is the rods' action. Action is a measurement of deflection or flex that the rod exhibits under load, and more importantly, where that flex occurs along the rod blank. "Extra Fast" action rods flex more towards the tip and are used when fishing light jigs, live bait or plastics. "Slow" action rods distribute the flex progressively throughout the entire rod blank and are desired when fishing crankbaits and spinnerbaits.

The next thing to consider is the rods' power. Power is defined by the amount of pressure required to flex the rod blank. Most rods are designed to optimally manage a specific range of lure and line weights. The heavier the line and lure, the more power you'll need to cast, fight and pull

effectively. The lighter the line and lure, the less power you will need.

When choosing a rod for topwater fishing anglers need to take into consideration both the action and the power of the rod as well as the weight of the lure. Many smallmouth anglers make the mistake of using a rod that has an action and power that is to light. They will complain about the light bite and are annoyed by all the missed fish and the thought that their favorite rod is not the proper tool for the job never enters their mind.

I will use a six foot six medium power spinning or casting rod with a fast tip when fishing smaller poppers and prop baits. If the tip is to stiff it will hinder the action of the lure but if the tip is to fast it will impair the hookset. When using larger prop baits or stick baits I prefer a six foot six rod with the same power but it should have a slower tip. The length of the rod is a personal preference and while I use six foot six inch rods if a longer seven foot rod is your preference, go for it.

Line

There is no go to line when fishing topwater baits. You will need to consider the lure you are using, type of water and type of structure. Under one situation eight pound monofilament will get the job done but in another situation you might need 20 pound braided line. This book will go into detail on which line is best for a particular situation. Choosing the right line is often a personal selection and if a specific line works well for you and gives you confidence, use it.

Adjust prop baits

There are times when you need a little more persuasion to trigger a strike. You don't need to change colors or switch to a larger bait but what is needed is to fine tune the prop. With a pair of ordinary fishing pliers you can GENTLY tweak the blades of the propellers on your lures to a sharper angle. This will cause more disturbances in the water. The opposite can hold true after a cold front when you might want to tweak your propellers create less disturbance in the water.

Fishing For Smallmouth Bass
Split rings

Should I add a split ring to the bait? The rule of thumb is that manufacturers package the lures the way they are intended to be used. Most of them are designed to impart their signature actions the way they come out of the package. So for the most part if it comes with a split ring – leave it on. On the other hand many anglers feel that if the lure does not have a split ring don't add one. That might be fine for largemouth bass but when it comes to smallmouth bass I will experiment with each individual lure. On some baits adding a split ring can result in a more solid hookset since the split ring will turn the bait as the smallmouth hammers it. On many other baits the split ring will allow the lure to be more versatile allowing the angler to tweak the lure during the retrieve. The conclusion is that the angler should be innovative and fine tune the bait if needed and there is nothing cut in stone.

Dressed treble hooks

When it comes to topwater lures for smallmouth bass, always have a dressing on your treble hooks. If the surface lure does not have one out of the package – ADD ONE!

While more dressing does not equate to catching more fish, there needs to be a noticeable amount present. After catching a boat load of fish the dressing needs to be replaced. To keep my sanity in the northwoods winter I will often spend a day replacing the frayed and bare rear treble hooks on my topwater lures. I will also carry a few dressed treble hooks in my topwater box for on the water repair. With the use a split ring pliers you can quickly add a fresh dressed treble and get the hot bit back in the water. The best dressed treble hooks will have a combination of dear hair and feathers. The dear hair should be short about even with the bottom of the treble hook. One or two feathers should hang down at least ¾ of an inch past the treble. There is no need to overdo it with the feather and hair dressing. For smallmouth I like to use white hair with a red feather. I have also had good success with chartreuse or yellow feathers.

Spinnerbaits

My clients will often ask me what the best spinnerbait color is and I usually respond that there is none. In my 30 some years of fishing and guiding, I have rarely seen a situation where largemouth bass only preferred one color. On many occasions I have seen colors on the opposite end of the spectrum catch big fish on the same water on the same day. If you stick with chartreuse, yellow and white in stained or dark water, and white, blue and black in clear water you can't go wrong.

Anglers should pay far more attention to the type and color of the blade on the spinnerbait than the color of the skirt. While there are some basic rules to follow when choosing spinnerbait blades, anglers will need to experiment with different blades on the different lakes they are fishing. The only thing for certain is that when fishing during the pre-spawn you should use smaller blades in gin clear water and larger blades in dark or muddy water.

In clear water I have had my best success with nickel willow leaf blades. Bass see well in clear water and the large willowleaf blades signal bait fish to a bass. The wide wobble of the willowleaf blade also emits intense vibrations which trigger veracious bass strikes in clear water. After a cold front I will switch to Colorado blades on my spinnerbaits.

Willow leaf blades will catch largemouth in stained and dark water but I have had my best success with Colorado blades. When fishing under stable and warming conditions tandem Colorado Blades are best. If you are fishing after a cold front, start fishing with a single blade spinnerbait.

Another common mistake made when fishing spinnerbaits is choosing the weight of the spinnerbait. I say this because the biggest selling spinnerbait is 1/4 ounce. If you look at what spinnerbaits most pro tournaments are won with, you will find that the baits are nearly always 3/8 ounce or larger. The reason for all this is that a 3/8 ounce, or heavier, bait is so much more versatile than a 1/4 ounce. A larger spinnerbait bait can be fished at any speed and run correctly. A 1/4 ounce bait will roll over or pop out of the water when fished at high speeds, which is my best tactic for water with good visibility. A 3/8 ounce bait can be fished at much greater depths when needed. A 1/4 ounce bait takes too long to get down to a desired depth, costing you casts over the course of a day. It simply will not stay near the bottom when trying to slow roll. You

IMPORTANT IDEA

will also lose contact with it when trying to fish deep. You are very limited with the blade sizes you can use with a 1/4 ounce. You can put any size on a 3/8 ounce or a 1/2 ounce.

Jigs

Another good tactic is jig fishing. Jig fishing catches big bass but fishing jigs *"properly"* is a difficult skill to master. The technique demands diligent focus and a delicate touch. This is one reason that as a guide I seldom use this presentation with my clients. It is much easier to fish soft plastics or even spinnerbaits. Many anglers will toss their fair share of jigs without any result and abandon the presentation.

Blade Baits

At first glance blade baits resemble jigging spoons. While they can in fact be used for vertical jigging they are best used with a cast and retrieve presentation. Like jigging spoons they will catch smallmouth in stained water but they shine in clear water.

Chapter 2
Structure

It is no secret that smallmouth relate to structure. While anglers have no trouble locating structure, the key is to locate structure that contains fish. But for many anglers this is easier said than done. It seems that every time I am on the water I will notice a few anglers fishing around some kind of structure. I would like to go over and tell them that they are wasting their time. They probably fished their favorite spot in the past and had good success, or maybe their grandfather told them it was a good spot. Whatever the reason, it might not be that they are fishing in a bad spot, but rather that they are just fishing in the wrong place at the wrong time.

One of the first things I learned was to not only remember the spot where I caught fish, but also the time of year and the conditions for that day. Before we get into the nuts and bolts on how to catch more smallmouth, it is important to understand structure basics.

Fishing For Smallmouth Bass

Generally, you will find most fish relating to some sort of structure. In order to better grasp how smallmouth will relate to structure the angler needs to understand the big picture and take all species into consideration. The only time when structure is not an issue is when predator fish are suspending over open water while feeding on forage fish. Most of the time both predator and prey are suspending at a desired water temperature. However, on many occasions fish that are suspending in the water column are in proximity to some type of structure.

On many lakes anglers can easily pick up clues as to the structure of the lake by gazing at the shoreline. A point piercing out from the shoreline will usually signal the presence of an underwater point breaking to deep water. A high steep bank usually indicates a steep drop-off along the shoreline. When a creek enters the lake or river the angler can assume there will be a soft muck bottom and schools of baitfish. So while it is essential that anglers always check out the obvious features on a lake or river, you must also learn not to take anything for granted. Nobody said locating fish was going to be easy.

I know of a few steep rock outcroppings that break into five feet of water. There is also more than one point that breaks towards the shoreline and comes to an abrupt end as it enters the water. On one section of my favorite river a small creek enters the river. It has "big fish" written all over it but all I ever caught there were a few bullheads and a carp. That is one spot that I am eager to share with any angler. Unfortunately, understanding and reading structure is no easy nut to crack, and it may take a great deal of time actually on the water to learn the structure of a specific body of water. On the bright side, there are a few tools that can increase your odds, but you need to accept that just because you find structure does not mean you will catch smallmouth.

Structure can be a number of things including rocks, wood, weeds, boat docks or any element in the water, natural or man-made. In the spring, smallmouth head for the shallows or move over shoreline points to spawn. After spawning is complete, fish either feed in weeds, head for deep water or hold tight to some type of structure. In summer, some smallmouth will stack up in the weeds while other fish move to mid lake humps, deep wood or points. In fall, the weeds continue to attract smallmouth, but eventually they migrate to deep cover. While smallmouth migrations are different on lakes, reservoirs and rivers, the one thing they all have in common is structure. So regardless of the season, the secret to catching more smallmouth is in understanding how smallmouth relate to structure during their seasonal migrations.

A successful angler will have the ability to zero in on the type of structure smallmouth will be using on any given day. The angler will need to take into consideration both the seasonal migrations and current weather and water conditions. What are the water temperature, water level and wind direction? Are we fishing during cold front conditions? While there are a few guidelines to follow, determining the *days' bite* is best ascertained, again, by time on the water.

While I have logged in thousands of hours on the water I don't rely on a lake map for most of the water that I fish. In fact, most of the time the only reason I turn on my electronics is to check the water temperature or see if fish are relating to a piece of structure, not to locate structure. However, if I am going to fish new water, the first thing I check out is a lake map. It is important to study the lake and mark out potential fishing areas before you head out on the water. During my downtime, of which there is far too much living here in the Northwoods, I spend countless hours studying both my favorite waters and potential places to fish during the upcoming season. I not only look for potential hot spots, I try to eliminate non-productive water. Eliminating bad water is just as important as finding hot spots. I don't depend on other anglers to lead me to where the fish are biting; I look for my own honey holes.

When looking at a lake map of a chosen lake, regardless of the size of the lake the first thing I look for is any outstanding features within the shoreline contour lines. Look for shallow bays and focus on where the bay breaks into deep water. Also look for any irregular breaks in the contour lines. Look for the contour lines that come tightly together; these indicate a steep drop-off. Contour lines that are far apart indicate a gradual slope. Understanding the contour of the lake you are fishing is as important as choosing the right lure.

Occasionally, sharp spikes in the contours appear on maps and can often look like mistakes. A wise angler will pay close attention to even the slightest variation in the contours. Even a small spike in the map might be a rock point or an abrupt change in the bottom content. I do not use a GPS and so on several lakes that I fish, these small spikes in the lakes' contours are hard to locate. Keep in mind that many lake maps are old and have not been updated, and abrupt changes in the contour can signal nothing at all.

Once you locate one of these small spots and catch some fish, the trick is to be able to return to the spot and catch more fish. Most of the time I can get close to the small spot by using both a locator and by lining the spot up with shoreline markers. These markers can be trees, rocks, cabins or boat docks. First, find the proper depth and then triangulate three separate markers in three different directions. You can log this on the map for further use. I would suggest writing this on your lake map as soon as possible since you can quickly forget your markers if you don't fish the lake regularly.

Over the years many of my clients are amazed at how quickly I can find fishing spots, but they do not realize that I am triangulating the spot. If anything I will make it look like the spot is harder to find. An old guide trick is to lead the client into thinking it is all the more difficult to locate fish. Actually, the more time you spend on the water the easier triangulating and locating fish becomes, at least most of the time.

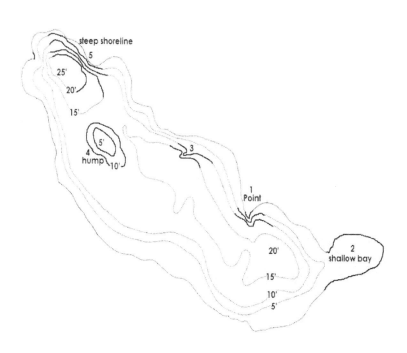

A good lake map is a must

Structure

After I get a handle on the overall contour of the lake, I next look for outstanding features within the map. An outstanding feature can be an off shore hump, an island or a shoreline point. On most lake maps off shore humps, regardless of their size, are easy to see on the map, but only large shoreline points are well defined. Once you find structure look for any variations within the contour within the structure. On any given piece of structure there will usually be one deep edge and one shallow edge.

Just when you think you have a lake figured out you will stumble on a new hot spot or fishing pattern. I have had many slow days on the water when, just as I was ready to throw in the towel, I found a minute change in the structure and caught a boat load of fish. Even on infertile natural lakes where structure is limited there is usually something different on the lake each year. The change can be a new fallen tree, new boat dock or a change in the weed growth. So if you are fishing on your favorite water and you are not having any success, there is no need to panic as long as you look for new structure.

Many lake maps today will have the GPS coordinates on specific pieces of structure. This will help anglers easily locate structure, or as I like to say, it takes all the fun out of it. As you examine the lake map keep in mind that even the best lake maps will miss small pieces of structure, and that many times these small pieces of structure can attract big fish. The fact that a spot is not on a map equates to limited fishing pressure. In fact, I spend a great deal of time searching for these out of the way places. These out of the way places become my "secret spots" that produce fish when the chips are down; you will learn to protect them as best you can.

After you locate your honey hole, a floating marker will aid you in relocating structure or fish. The problem with most floating markers available on the market today is that they are too large. While they are easy to locate for the angler, they are also visible to every other angler on the lake. As a guide, the last thing I want to do is advertise where I am catching fish. I have enough problems with anglers following me around the lake. In order to solve this problem I learned long ago to make my own floating markers. I would take a three inch piece of Styrofoam, paint it black, attach some nylon string and tie on a weight to the end of the line. I would toss out the small marker when I found a desired piece of structure. By marking the spot with this small black marker I was pretty much assured that no other angler would find it, but I could return to the spot later in the day or the next day if need be. Of course, this was in my younger years when my eyesight was much better.

Fishing For Smallmouth Bass

Regardless of the time of year there is usually some sort of fish activity centered on an off shore hump. Each lake is different depending on it size, available forage, water quality and dominant predator fish. All these factors will determine what kind of fish will relate to the structure and when they will move onto the structure.

Early in the season I concentrate my efforts on humps that are at or just below the surface. A shallow hump that is less than 10 feet in depth will see a variety of fish species. Smallmouth will use a shallow hump to spawn provided suitable spawning habitat is present. Even if only one species of fish uses the hump to spawn, it will attract other predator fish looking for an easy meal. During the early season, deep water humps will attract large predator fish, but they are inactive. Later in summer deeper humps can be the key to catching more and bigger fish.

The ideal early season hump will rise out of moderate depth water and not be far from a shallow bay. The shallowest hump in the lake or reservoir will have the warmest water and attract the most species of fish. A hump that rises out of deep water in the middle of the lake might attract spawning walleyes but not other species. After spawning, big walleyes will hold along the deep edges of the hump and so will big post-spawn northern pike and muskies.

If you are looking for consistent fishing action look for a hump that has a mix of rock, soft bottom and weeds. Diagram "A" shows the type of off shore hump that will attract a variety of different types of fish from spring through fall. While rocks are the main element of the hump, the sand allowed for the weeds to take root. The combination of weeds and rocks attract baitfish and crayfish. During the day smallmouth can feed on the hump and walleyes will move onto the hump after dark. Perch will relate to the deep rock and weed transition area. Transition areas are where the bottom changes from one type of bottom to another type of bottom. Perch will also move shallow to feed in the weeds at any time. A musky or northern pike can also be present. At any given time there is some kind of fish activity centered around the hump, although the feeding movements are tough to pattern.

Diagram B shows a hump that tops out at 10 feet that is made up entirely of rock. These are the type of humps that are most productive from mid-summer through late fall. Smallmouth will relate to the top of the hump during the day and when they are not on the hump they could be suspending off the edges. Walleyes will feed on small perch and minnows during low light conditions and during the day hold tight to the rocks or hold in deep water.

The ledge along the first break of the hump acts as a holding area primarily for walleyes and an occasional smallmouth bass. This ledge would be impossible to find with a locator. The problem is that a rock ledge can be erratic and while a locator will show the actual ledge, walleye holding tight to the ledge can avoid electronics. A smart angler will fish the ledge with a fine tooth comb. The tighter fish hold to the rocks the slower an angler will need to fish.

In mid-summer it is important to know when to fish a specific hump. On a typical hump you can expect to find walleye and smallmouth feeding early and late in the day. At night walleyes will dominate the structure. When walleyes are inactive they will hold tight to deeper structure while smallmouth will suspend off the edge of the hump. A musky can be found in the area at any time. If the musky is not feeding on the hump it could suspend off the edge of the hump or move to deep water. In general, most feeding occurs during low light conditions. Low light conditions are at night, evenings, mornings and overcast days.

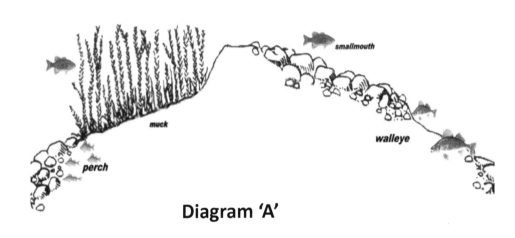

Diagram 'A'

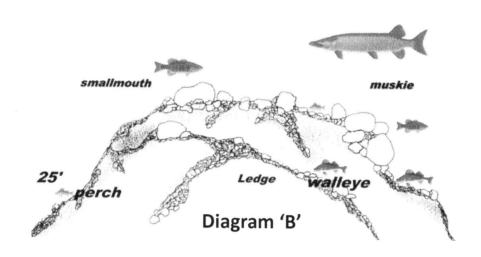

smallmouth

muskie

25'

Ledge

walleye

perch

Diagram 'B'

Points

Most anglers have trouble finding a shoreline point for the first time unless it is an outstanding feature on the lake. The problem is that if the point is an outstanding feature on a lake it may be too easy to locate, making it a popular gathering place for anglers. Anglers that follow the crowds and fish the local favorite honey hole which has seen every lure including the kitchen sink usually do not fare very well. Sure, living up to its reputation, a fair share of fish are caught there each year, but I need some elbow room when fishing.

I like to search for secondary points since they are not on a map and will require effort to locate them. The more difficult a point is to find the lighter the fishing pressure will be. However, just because you locate a shoreline point does not mean you will catch fish. Once an angler locates a point, finding fish and figuring out how to fish the point can be a complex issue. The angler needs to take into consideration the dominant species in the lake, available forage species, water temperature and bottom content. It is not as simple as positioning your boat over the point and tossing out a bobber. If it was that simple, there would be no need for fishing guides and I would have to look for a real job.

A point, like every other piece of structure, can be visited by a variety of fish species at the same time, or the point might see periodic movements of one particular species. Over the years I have watched anglers fish a point for one species of fish only to catch another once they find a different species on the prowl. If this happens more than once, the angler usually deletes the point from his list of choice fishing spots. If the angler had fished the point at a different time of day, the point might be at the top of his list. Just as when fishing an off shore hump, they fail to understand the pecking order.

One prime example was a point that I have regularly fished throughout the years which is probably my favorite point. In my 30 years as a professional fishing guide my clients have caught limits of walleyes, 6 pound smallmouth, 40 inch northern pike, wallhanger muskies, bluegill, perch and crappie. It is one of those spots that no matter what type of conditions I have to deal with, I can usually produce a few quality fish.

After fishing the point for over 30 years I was able to pattern when a specific specie would be most active. These patterns include the time of the feeding periods and what species would be most active under specific weather patterns. I also know when to avoid the point and fish elsewhere. While it is far from an exact science, my pattern for fishing the point is about 80 percent accurate, which is about as good as any anglers' prediction.

After ice out, large predator fish will hold tight and suspend off the deeper edges of the point. Any boulders are magnets for trophy walleye, pike, smallmouth bass and muskies. Walleyes will spawn on the point in spring and, after spawning, move atop a small rock hump off the deep edge of the point. Early in the day they will move atop the point to feed on minnows, but once the light penetrates through the dark water they head back for the hump. A few hours later the dark water warms up a few degrees and big smallmouth invade the point as they search out their spawning sites. As evening approaches smallmouth back off from the shallows and the walleyes return. If the sun remains behind the clouds, walleyes fan out across the point during the day and I look for the big smallmouth to hold off the deep edge of the point or atop the rock hump.

By early summer once smallmouth spawning is complete, bluegill move into the shallows, crappie will suspend off the emerging weeds and a few largemouth bass will spawn tight to downed shoreline wood. Walleyes will feed both on the point and in the weeds at dawn and dusk, while smallmouth are relating to the hump. After walleyes complete their feeding binge they switch places with the smallmouth and head to their favorite hump off the deep edge of the point. Bluegill will be most active in the weeds early in the day and crappie suspending off the weeds are most active at dusk. If you are looking for perch, concentrate on the base of the weeds early and late in the day.

Shorline Point

Many anglers believe that just because they are fishing during overcast skies that the fish will jump into the boat. Nothing can be further from the truth. If the overcast skies are a result of a passing cold front with northwest winds, it will be a tough bite. Like clockwork, smallmouth would hold tight to the top of the hump, the walleyes congregate along the deep edge of the hump, largemouth and bluegills will bury themselves in the weeds, crappie will suspend over open water and muskies could end up anywhere. Smallmouth and walleye can be caught, but it will require persistence and a good sense of feel. Of all the species I have fished over the past thirty years, largemouth bass were the most predictable, and a well-placed jig could result in a five pounder.

If you are lucky enough to experience overcast days during an approaching warm front you can count on an excellent day on the water. Walleye and smallmouth will roam the weed-lines throughout the day and on many occasions my clients would catch limits of walleyes and a hoard of smallmouth without moving the boat for an extended period of time. We would normally catch walleyes on one side of the boat and smallmouth on the other since one species would be foraging in the weeds and the other in the staging area. This is *not* a good day to be a baitfish. On more than one outing the highlight of the day was a big musky biting off my client's favorite lure.

In fall, my favorite point continues to hold a variety of predator fish but the feeding windows are smaller. Walleye action still peaks early and late in the day but smallmouth bass and largemouth bass are most active from 10 am until 2 pm. Bluegill and crappie also feed regularly during mid-day and a musky could appear at any time. These feeding patterns hold true regardless of the weather conditions.

Transition areas have been my little secret for years. They are those places that are off the beaten path, and while they might not hold the most fish, they hold big fish. My clients have boated countless trophy fish off transition areas without having a clue as to why the fish were holding there. Not that I don't share my expertise with my clients, but for the most part the client is so thrilled about the big fish that they don't pursue the logistics. That is not to say that, even if they do inquire as to why the big fish was in that particular spot, that I don't come up with some sort of cockamamie answer.

You see, your typical transition area can be difficult to locate and I can easily confuse the savviest of anglers as I locate the spot. I again use the old guide trick of taking several minutes longer than needed to locate a spot. This added time makes a big fish all the more appreciated and the day could end up with a nice tip for the guide.

Basically, a transition area is simply a change from one type of bottom content to another. Pre-spawn smallmouth are notorious for staging in a hard bottom-soft bottom transition. The smallmouth will spawn on the hard bottom but the hard bottom warms slower than the soft bottom. As the big female smallmouth cruise the warm water they hit a bulkhead of cooler water as they enter their hard bottom spawning areas. The smaller male smallmouth might continue to move onto the spawning areas but the females stack up along the transition.

Smallmouth seldom relate to transition areas in summer with the exception being a severe cold front. As the water temperatures drop in fall and smallmouth begin to stack up they head for transitions. Whatever type of water you are fishing, a stop at a transition is a must.

Fishing For Smallmouth Bass

Rock/Sand Transition Area

Chapter 3
Forage

Knowing the main forage base on the water you are fishing can be a big part of the puzzle. Aside from the spawning period, forage will dictate the location of smallmouth bass. You can have the best looking structure, but if the restaurant is not open, nobody will be home. In order to catch more fish an angler needs to be aware of what is on the menu. Far too many anglers start out on a new lake and cast their favorite lure that works on their favorite lake, not realizing that it could be totally foreign to the local inhabitants.

When I fish new water, I will spend as much time researching the waters' dominate forage base as studying the structure. Let's face it, if fish are aggressive, they will hit anything that is thrown at them. The reality is that most fish, particularly the larger ones, acquire a preference for certain menus. Big predator fish are persnickety, but if you can match the menu at their favorite restaurant the odds will turn in your favor. One of the tricks I have learned in my 30 plus years of guiding is that by knowing the habits of the forage I am able to outsmart the prey.

Minnows

There are over 200 minnow species in North America. Now before you panic, there is no need to learn them all. You do not need to know the number of fin rays and the scale count of the various species. We can leave that to the fish biologists. However, the angler needs to be aware of the dominant minnow species in the geographical location and which specie is the preferred forage on the particular water they are fishing.

Shiners

There are several sub-species of shiners in North America. The golden shiner is probably the most recognizable minnow species to anglers since they are found in most bait shops. The golden shiner is a medium-sized minnow that has a deep slab-sided body. Young golden shiners lack the golden color, but possess a dusky lateral band that fades with age. They are often silvery in appearance, becoming dark golden as they age. Adults are usually 3-7 inches in length, with specimens occasional reaching 10 inches.

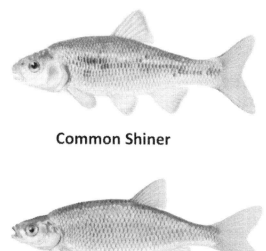

Common Shiner

Golden Shiner

This minnow occupies a wide range in the eastern half of the United States from Manitoba and Quebec and southward to Florida and Mexico. It has also been widely introduced west of the Rocky Mountains. Golden shiners are found in both stained and clear water lakes, rivers and reservoirs. They are usually found in schools and it is common to see schools of shiners breaking the surface as they suspend off of weed lines. Rarely do golden shiners suspend over open water. The food of the golden shiner consists largely of planktonic crustaceans, aquatic insects, mollusks, and algae. They are easily raised in controlled environments making them ideal for bait dealers. They are the bait of choice for ice fishing.

While golden shiners are found in rivers and small streams, the common shiner or river shiner is usually the most abundant forage. The common shiner resembles the golden shiner except the body is slimmer and the snout is rounded, making it more adaptable to moving water. The common shiner averages 6 inches long and can occasionally reaches 8 inches. The common shiner feeds extensively on both terrestrial and aquatic insects. When river shiners are on the feed, predator fish are not far behind.

The creek chub is a medium sized minnow with a single small barbell near the end of each jaw. There are several sub-species and the color can range from bluish to olive above and lighter colors below. The creek chub has a large mouth, with the upper jaw reaching to or beyond the front of the eye. The creek chub is widely distributed from the Rocky Mountains to eastern Canada and south to the Gulf of Mexico. The adult creek chub is usually 3-8 inches in length. Creek chubs are important forage in streams and rivers.

Creek Chub

Red Tail Chub

Redtail chubs are native to clear streams of the Upper Midwest. They prefer shallow water flowing over gravel. Redtail chubs have become increasingly appealing as walleye and smallmouth bass bait as both species pig out on them in the fall. Unfortunately for anglers, prices have escalated while their abundance in the wild has diminished. Additionally, bait dealers and anglers have noticed that it is more difficult to purchase this prized minnow. The redtail chubs they buy are smaller than they were several years ago, possibly reflecting harvesting pressure. Anglers can pay as much as $8 a dozen for red tail chubs making them more expensive per pound than lobster. Proto-type aquaculture systems were developed for spawning and raising redtail chubs and hopefully, like golden shiners they will be raised in hatcheries for future live bait anglers.

Blacktail chubs are more abundant than red tail chubs in many areas and they are a viable alternative bait. I have used black tail chubs on rivers and have found no difference in my catch rate when compared to using red tail chubs. However, on clear water natural lakes I feel that red tail chubs will catch bigger fish than black tail chubs, but use whatever is available.

The fathead minnow is a small olive colored minnow with a lateral line that seldom exceeds 3 inches. A narrow, dark vertical bar is often present at the base of the caudal fin. Together with several sub-species, the fathead minnow is widespread from southern Canada, east of the Rocky Mountains to Maine, and southward to the Susquehanna River and to the Gulf States. In northern waters the fatheads prefer lakes, reservoirs, rivers and streams and are important forage for walleye, bass, and small pike. They are the ideal forage for young predator fish. The fathead feeds extensively on microscopic algae as well as other plankton. An easily propagated species, the fathead is popular with commercial hatcheries, which raise them for both bait and for forage in ponds.

The white sucker is the most common sucker specie due to its tolerance of a variety of conditions. This olive-brown sucker prefers mid-sized to large rivers, reservoirs and deep lakes. It is also at home in both fast and sluggish streams and thick weed cover. It is also tolerant of large amounts of pollution, siltation, and turbidity and is able to survive in waters of low oxygen. White suckers feed on a variety of foods, including aquatic insect larva, crustaceans, mollusks, and algae. The white sucker usually runs 10-20 inches in length.

The soft and bony fish moves slowly along the bottom and is easy prey for predators. In fall northern pike and muskie feed heavily on white suckers. Smaller suckers are also popular bait for walleyes and smallmouth bass.

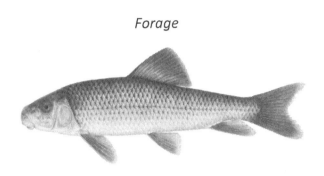

The northern redhorse sucker is found in the north and central states east of the Rockies and throughout central and eastern Canada. It is a clean water species found in rivers, streams and lakes and can't tolerate even low levels of pollution. The young feed on minute plankton until they are large enough to begin the adult diet of insect larva and small mollusks, which are sucked from the gravel and rock bottom. They are often found feeding alongside smallmouth bass, walleye and sturgeon. They can grow up to 24 inches and weigh up to 10 pounds. Northern pike and muskie will feed on the adult specimens, while walleye and smallmouth bass feed on juveniles.

Another important sucker specie for predator fish is the hog sucker. It has a large head, with a depression between the eyes and a sucking-type mouth, and 4 dark oblique bars on the body. The eyes are behind the middle of the snout. The whole body appears almost conical and is covered with large scales. Some hog suckers attain a length of 2 feet, but 10-12 inches is the usual size.

The northern hog sucker is found from central Minnesota eastward through the Great lakes region to New York, down the Mississippi drainage to the Gulf of Mexico. It is generally present only in clear rivers and streams. Preferred habitats are riffles and areas adjacent to clear, shallow streams with gravel or rock bottoms. It also frequents the shallow areas of lakes near the mouth of a creek or river. Smallmouth bass and walleye prey on the hog sucker. They are a popular bait since they are easily trapped. A hog sucker rigged on a quick strike rig can produce a wall hanger muskie in fall.

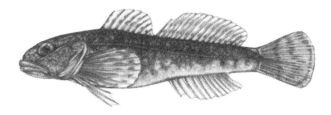

Sculpins are small fish with species varying in size from 2-30 inches. This odd looking fish is distinguished by a bony support extending under the skin from the cheek to the eye. The head is large and depressed; the eyes are high and closely set and the gill membranes are connected. The environment has an effect on its coloration. Sculpins are important forage for gamefishes, particularly trout and smallmouth bass. On occasion they are used as bait.

There are 11 North American species in this group of lake-inhabiting members of the Salmonidae family. Ciscoes are also called tullibee and lake herring because they resemble herrings in outward appearance. They are white or silvery to blue in color and range in size from 6-20 inches, but some species have been reported up to 7 pounds. All ciscoes are cold water fishes, occurring from New England through the Great Lakes into Canada. They feed on planktonic crustaceans and bottom-dwelling insects and can be found in shallow water and at depths over 100 feet. Most of the year they suspend over open water at various depths in the water column. They are an important forage for salmon, trout, northern pike, muskie, walleye and smallmouth bass. Ciscoes spawn in November over hard bottom. Locate spawning ciscoes and you will also locate large predator fish.

Whitefish are another member of the Salmonidae family and are larger than the cisco. They have many of the same habits of the cisco. In the great lakes they are forage for salmon, trout, muskies, northern pike and walleye.

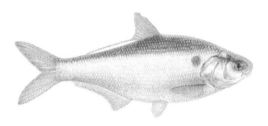

Shad are members of the Herring Family and most of them are anadromous fish, ascending coastal waters to spawn. The gizzard shad is not a migratory shad and tends to stay in the same locality throughout the year. It is a deep-bodied species, generally silver with bluish above and brassy to reddish reflections on the side. The gizzard shad inhabits fresh and brackish water, in bays, lakes, bayous, and large rivers, regardless of the water clarity. It is wide-spread from the Mississippi River and its drainage, from Minnesota south to the Gulf of Mexico, and from New Jersey southward. Adults can reach a length of 16 inches but they seldom exceed 12 inches.

The gizzard shad feeds on small organisms which it strains from the mud with its gillrakers. Most of its food is made up of plant material and organic debris. The food is ground in the gizzard like stomach and long intestine. Because of this apparatus, the species is extremely important as a forage fish, converting organic matter and plant material directly to fish flesh, which then becomes food for predator fish. The gizzard shad is an important forage for largemouth bass, striped bass and white bass. In some waters the gizzard shad has created a serious management problem due to its extreme abundance where no large predator population exists. The gizzard shad is a poor live bait because it dies quickly on a hook and it is hard to keep alive even in an aerated live well.

Crayfish

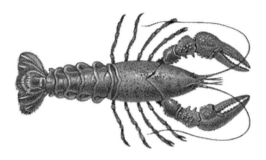

Fishing For Smallmouth Bass

There are over 350 species of crayfish in North America. Crayfish are at home in small streams, big rivers and lakes and are an important part of the food chain. They are a major food source for both largemouth and smallmouth bass which lead to the design of many soft plastic baits. Many color patterns were developed to match a specific crayfish species in a particular body of water.

Crayfish are either male or female but it is not uncommon to find individuals with both male and female genital openings; in most instances these crayfish are found to be male. Generally, breeding occurs in spring with actual the spawning time being determined by the species of crayfish and geographical location.

As they prepare to spawn, crayfish will respond both to the water temperature and light penetration. In many locations crayfish will spawn more than once. In tropical waters crayfish can breed all year round because their temperature environment is more stable. Unlike saltwater crayfish, freshwater crayfish have large eggs and they are 'mothered' by the female for a period after birth.

Eggs stay on the tail for at least four weeks for warmer water species and much longer for the cold water species. There are also other variables such as food and water conditions which can effect this gestation period. In northern waters this gestation period could linger until late June.

Once hatched, young crayfish cling to the female's swimmerets for three to four molts (molting is when crayfish shed their old shell to allow growth). Young crayfish may stay with the female for several weeks. She offers them protection during this vulnerable life stage. Eventually, the young leave the female. They undergo eight to ten molts before they mature, which may occur during the first year, but more likely in the following year.

Crayfish are considered opportunistic feeders. Rusty crayfish feed on a variety of aquatic plants, benthic invertebrates (like aquatic worms, snails, leeches, clams, aquatic insects, and crustaceans such as side-swimmers and water fleas), detritus (decaying plants and animals, including associated bacteria and fungi), fish eggs, and small fish. Juveniles in particular will feed on benthic invertebrates like mayflies, stoneflies, midges, and side-swimmers.

I have witnessed smallmouth bass foraging on crayfish until the water temperature drops below 45 degrees. Once the water temperature drops below 40 degrees crayfish move into their winter pattern. During this period some species of crayfish will dig burrows while others will crawl tight under a rock where they will remain until spring arrives.

Hellgrammites

Hellgrammites are the larvae of the dobsonfly, a rather large insect (2 to 4 inches long) with large, mottled wings that are held flat over the back and extend beyond the abdomen when at rest. The males have long, extended curved mandibles that are used to grasp the female during mating. The aquatic larvae are elongated (about the same size as the adult), dull colored, and have gill filaments and gill clusters along the sides of the abdomen. They have two hooks on the end of the abdomen. Most notable on the hellgrammite is the large jaw that is used to grasp prey in the water. Adult dobsonflies probably do not feed, as their long mandibles (especially the males) would make it very hard to eat. The hellgrammites on the other hand, are voracious predators that attack other aquatic insects and other organisms. Most of the dobsonfly's life cycle is spent in the larval stage in well-oxygenated, high quality water. Hellgrammites can be found in riffle areas of streams, hiding among rocks. Hellgrammites are a favorite food for many fish, including smallmouth bass, rock bass, perch and catfish. Because of this they are often collected for fish bait. As mentioned before, hellgrammites are fierce biters, but are not dangerous. Hellgrammites are very sensitive to water pollution.

Leeches

Fish eat many types of leeches, but only the ribbon leech is widely used as bait. Ribbon leeches will not suck your blood. They have a small suction cup which they use as a foot; this allows them to anchor themselves while feeding. Ribbon leeches feed primarily at night when they feed on mosquito larva and decaying organic matter and are rarely seen during the daytime. Because leeches can be easily transported and require little care, they have become a premium walleye and bass bait.

Ribbon or bait leeches are available in jumbo, extra large, large and medium. Leeches are sold by weight because of their ability to stretch out. A jumbo leech when flat is about 2 inches long, when it stretches out it may be 6 inches long. A large leech is about 1-2 inches flat and 4 1/2 inches stretched out. A medium is about 1 inch flat and 2 1/2 inches stretched out. A small leech is about 1/2 inch flat and 1 inch stretched out. These are only approximate numbers as all leeches are different. The picture below is of a handful of jumbo leeches.

Clear water that is free from chlorine is necessary for maintaining leeches. Avoid placing leeches in chlorinated water. Leeches are sensitive to substances such as chlorine, copper, and other chemicals. Non-chlorinated tap water in most areas is suitable for leeches. Do not use distilled water alone since its extreme purity can be harmful to the leeches' metabolic balance. Keep the water clean. Once the water shows signs of becoming dirty or polluted, it should be changed.

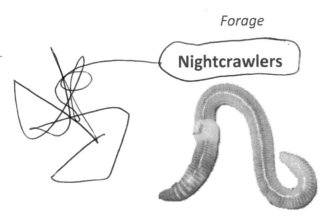

Nightcrawlers

Nightcrawlers and other worm types are as close as you can get to a universal live bait for all species of freshwater fish. They will catch any fish from common bluegill to sturgeon. Fishing nightcrawlers have amazing fish appeal but there are some important reasons they are so popular. They are a very easy bait to find and a very easy bait to catch or raise. After a good rain you can catch enough worms for multiple fishing trips. You can keep nightcrawlers alive for weeks at a time with some simple preparation. When you catch or buy your nightcrawlers make sure you put them in a large container, like a 5 gallon bucket. Fill the bucket at least 1/2 full with rich moist soil then keep them in a cool spot. Commercial worm bedding placed in a Styrofoam cooler, kept in a cool area or refrigerated will keep nightcrawlers through the season.

Nose hook crawlers and do not thread them. Go through the nose one time; when hooked, the tip of the crawler's nose should be behind the hook point.

The garden worm is often confused with a nightcrawler and is considered the most common fishing worm. Garden worms are also called angle worms. They are normally 3 to 4 inches in length and vary in color from pink to gray to bluish. They have a collar that is only slightly darker than their bodies.

Chapter 4
Pre-Spawn

    Most of my expertise with pre-spawn smallmouth is in northern waters and not the deep clear water reservoirs of the mid-south. In the north, smallmouth inhabit natural lakes, rivers and reservoirs. While they all contain smallmouth they must be approached with a different game plan. They can spend as much as 4 or 5 months in a period of inactivity due to hard water, so, when the ice finally leaves, smallmouth anglers head for their favorite water and find smallmouth that are not necessarily eager to chase their lures.

Fishing For Smallmouth Bass

In my home area of northern Wisconsin, I am unable to fish for smallmouth until the first week of May when the catch and release season opens. This is usually a few weeks after ice out. The water temperature is usually between 40-45 degrees when I catch my first smallmouth of the season. The typical pre-spawn pattern is to work the shallows looking for active smallmouth. If conditions are just right the angler can be very successful locating fish and have a great day on the water. However, there is never a sure thing when you are fishing, especially during the early season.

The pre-spawn bite is most unpredictable until the water temperature rises into the low 50 degree range. At that time there is a major movement into the shallows by both male and female smallmouth . When the water temperature hovers in the mid fifties the bite can get fantastic as water temperatures tend to hold steady overnight, even on those cold spring nights.

A cold front will push smallmouth off the spawning areas and on some waters this unfortunately means deep water. If I am hit with a cold front the first few weeks of the season I will concentrate on stained water reservoirs or rivers while avoiding deep clear natural lakes. Clear water lakes take longer to warm and anything that disrupts the rise in water temperature can spell disaster for even the most seasoned bass fisherman. That is why I keep stressing that the key to success in spring is fishing the water where you have the best chance of finding active fish.

If you want to connect with active smallmouth after ice out your best bet is to fish a small stained water reservoir. By small to mid-sized reservoirs I am referring to reservoirs under 2,000 acres. Stained water will warm quicker than clear water and smallmouth activity can be weeks ahead of a clear water reservoir or natural lake. Smaller reservoirs also tend to be shallow with more flats as opposed to steep shoreline breaks common on larger reservoirs.

Due to both its size and structure, the smaller the reservoir the easier it will be to put together a fishing pattern. Even if smallmouth are scattered and you're under the most adverse conditions you can usually locate a few smallmouth. On a smaller reservoir, prime pre-spawn structure can also be at a premium and once you locate that structure you will be on fish.

The amount of water flowing through the reservoir will have as much of an impact on stimulating smallmouth activity as the water temperature. Even if the water temperatures remain in the 40 degree range, snow melt or heavy rain will increase the flow of water through the reservoir. This increased flow will push smallmouth out of their wintering areas away from the current. It is important to understand that in spring smallmouth like to avoid the current.

Once smallmouth leave the deep water they will stage close to the actual spawning areas. The first place I elect to fish is the area around the dam. In winter there is minimal current moving through the reservoir and big smallmouth will stack up tight to deep wood and rocks. As the flow through the reservoir starts to increase, the big smallmouth will move out of the deep water and look for a comfort zone away from the current. The water temperatures can be under 40 degrees and smallmouth are not even close to entering the pre-spawn.

Rip rap shorelines adjacent to the dam can be excellent areas to start your hunt for big pre- spawn smallmouth. When the water temperature is below 40 degrees this is the only place where I can consistently catch big smallmouth. Rip rap shorelines have salvaged many a cold windy May day, keeping many a client happy.

The truth is that most anglers know that fishing during the pre-spawn can be unpredictable but they don't realize how tough it is for the guide. The clients show up, dressed for the elements and hope the guide can put them on big fish and make a big smallmouth magically end up on the end of their line. There have been many spring days when the only reason I am in the boat is because of paying clients. That said there has been many a day when I left the boat landing faced with deplorable conditions just hoping that a client could catch at least one big fish, only to have a banner day.

One of my most memorable pre-spawn days was under extreme conditions. The fishing season had opened a few days before and I had been fishing everyday with limited success. We boated quality smallmouth but we were unable to connect with any numbers or put together a pattern. The wind had been bellowing out of the northwest for several days and there was no weather change in sight. I was unable to fish my favorite dam and rip rap shoreline due to the 25 mph winds.

When I jumped in the truck in the morning and headed out to pick up my clients I noticed that the wind had shifted and was blowing out of the west. It was a sign of relief and I was hoping that just maybe I could get into my favorite spot. As I launched the boat I noticed that the wind was still blowing out of the west and I was hoping I could get in a few hours before the wind shifted out of the north like the weatherman had predicted. After all, the weatherman is never wrong.

Fishing For Smallmouth Bass

As we approached the dam I had one of my clients tie on a 1/4 ounce unpainted leadhead jig dressed with a three inch curly tail grub and the other tie on a 1/4 ounce chartreuse leadhead jig. I positioned my boat parallel to the rip rap shoreline and slowly moved the boat into the wind along the shoreline. I instructed the client with the grub to cast tight to the shoreline and slowly retrieve the grub back to the boat with an occasional pause. I dressed the chartreuse jig with a lively fathead minnow. I told him to watch me as I let the jig and minnow drop to the bottom and vertically jigged it about one foot off the bottom.

When I am guiding I seldom head for the honey hole right away. I like to get the feel of my clients and get them focused before we get on fish, but not knowing how long the wind would cooperate I knew I had to get on the fish ASAP. Well, let me tell you the rip rap played right into my game plan. There was a slight chop and the sun was a welcomed sight. I felt a strike on the drop with the jig and minnow but, being a good guide, I refrained from setting the hook. I quickly reeled up the jig and gave the rod to my client. As he let the jig drop I told him if he felt a strike to slowly lift the line and when he felt weight to set the hook. He was a quick learner and after he set the hook it was only a short time before I netted a 19 inch smallmouth.

After a few photos we released the smallmouth and I repositioned the boat right over the spot where we my client had caught the last smallmouth. It took a while but my client eventually connected with another dandy smallmouth. I explained to my clients that I found this pattern years ago while walleye fishing. The guy casting the grub did not even get a tap so I set him up with the same jig and minnow. Needless to say he also began catching 19 inch smallmouth. After the first hour we boated 20 smallmouth between 18 and 20 inches, which is excellent in anyone's book.

However, all good things must come to an end. The weather suddenly turned for the worse. The clouds moved in and the wind shifted from the west to the northwest and white caps soon consumed the rip rap. These conditions would have been okay in the fall, but not during the pre-spawn with 40 degree water temperatures. We tried using heavier jigs but only managed to stick one more smallmouth. The fish were still on the screen but they definitely had a case of lockjaw. We spent the rest of the day fishing every hot spot on the reservoir and we even took a drive up-river. We only managed to catch two more 15 inch smallmouth. I can only think what would have happened if the weather man had been wrong. Why is he always right when you don't want him to be right?

Another memorable guide trip was when my clients and I were hit with a horrendous cold front after summer like conditions had prevailed for about a week. Prior to the cold front the smallmouth went wild as they cruised the shallows. However, the water temperature had dropped six degrees in 2 days and the shallows were void of life. I had some clients that wanted to catch fish, and I knew I would have to pool all my resources the next few days.

We hit the water and the first thing that I noticed was a brisk northeast wind which is never a good wind in the spring. The water temperature was 49 degrees and I did not expect it to rise much during the day due to the northeast wind. I am no meteorologist but after spending thousands of days in a boat, I can predict weather with the best of them. The only positive factor that entered the picture was that there was not a cloud in the sky and I hoped that even if the morning was slow, by mid-day a slight climb in the water temperature might trigger smallmouth activity. It is important to always have a positive attitude when fishing.

For the first three hours my clients tried every lure in my bag of tricks but the only smallmouth brought to the boat was a 12 incher caught on a 1/16 ounce jig and a fathead minnow. I was actually getting a bit desperate, not just in my choice of lures but in my lack of locating smallmouth. One of my clients grabbed a five inch, bright orange deep diving crankbait out of his tackle box and asked me if I thought it would work. Even though I knew the crankbait was too large and wide for catching smallmouth under these conditions, I gave him a nod hoping he would catch a big northern pike.

I commented to my clients that it was starting to warm up, noting that the wind had died down. I looked at my electronics and noticed that the water temperature was now 52 degrees. Next, with the aid of my electric trolling motor, I moved the boat towards a large rock island where the only bronzeback of the day had been caught. Watching my electronics I suddenly saw several large arcs suspending about 2 feet off the bottom in 12 feet of water. We fished the area earlier in the day but we did not mark any fish on the locator. Where they came from I'll never know. Did they move into the area or were they holding tight to the rocks earlier in the day? One thing was for certain: there was no doubt in my mind that the recent spike in water temperature had something to do with it.

A small rock lip was on the edge of the main river channel and it was a staging area for pre-spawn smallmouth. The smallmouth were stacked up as they were waiting for the water to continue to warm. I told one of my clients to tie on a white Case Salted Minnow and instructed him to cast it out, let it sink for about 10 seconds, give it a short twitch and again let the minnow drop. I also told him that it was important to let the smallmouth engulf the bait for a few seconds before setting the hook. It did not take long for my client to yell, "Fish on!" However, in a few seconds his line went limp. I told him that he had set the hook too quickly and that when the smallmouth drops the bait, he should stop and let the bait fall for a few seconds. If the same smallmouth does not come back and hit the bait, there is a high probability that another smallmouth will. This deadly tactic allowed us to catch 17 smallmouth over 18 inches with the largest one being a big female that measured 21 inches. This was no accident. We were fishing in the right place at the right time with a bit of help from the sun and the lack of wind.

Most anglers can figure out where the smallmouth spawn but they have trouble locating the staging areas, which dictates their poor fishing. They will pound the shallows with a variety of baits not realizing that the pot of gold is only a short distance from their boat. The difference between a successful day on the water and getting skunked is not necessarily in the anglers' choice of bait but in their choice of location.

On stained water reservoirs these staging areas are the first transition area from the spawning beds. The transition area can be a transition from rock to sand or muck, a drop off to deep water, a few stumps or scattered weeds. Just prior to the actual spawn these areas can be stacked with big females on their way to the beds. If the big smallmouth are on the spawning beds they will return to these staging areas after a cold front.

When smallmouth are in the staging areas waiting for the water to warm, they will scatter and be on the prowl. At this time smallmouth will often suspend half way between the bottom and the surface and will respond to a variety of presentations. Since they are scattered the angler will need to keep on the move until he finds a concentration of fish. Once you connect with one fish, slow down because more are nearby.

A cold front will push smallmouth off the spawning beds and back to the staging areas. The difference will be that these smallmouth pushed off the spawning areas will hold tight to cover and the bottom. Anglers can scan the area with their electronics and with smallmouth being tight to cover they assume the area does not hold any fish. What I do is forget about my electronics and fish the staging areas, concentrating on cover. Slow down and work the cover with a fine tooth comb.

As I previously mentioned, the Case Sinking Minnow is my favorite bait for staging smallmouth. I have also had exceptional success with suspending jerkbaits with my favorite being the Yo-Zuri Edge Minnow. The edge Minnow is a universal minnow shape with a twist; it has three sides cut into it. The shape of the edger creates specific angles which reflect light into many different directions like the facets of a gem. The holographic foil adds to the attraction looking like scales falling off a wounded minnow. They also cut through the water like a knife creating a hard "slicing" action allowing you to switch direction on a dime. In any water conditions this looks like an escaping minnow. When retrieved fast the Edge Minnow has a wide wobble; when retrieved at a medium rate it has a wobbling roll, and when a slow retrieve is used it has a slow, tight rolling action. When suspended the Edge Minnow is at its best at enticing vicious strikes.

Another great suspending jerkbait from Yo-Zuri is the Sashimi. The Sashimi jerkbait can be used with a stop and go retrieve and / or a twitching motion. It is the only jerkbait available that continues to attract fish even when you stop your retrieve. It actually rocks back and forth when stopped and once this action has subsided, the added feather tail hook continues to pulsate, looking like a real fish's tail moving. While all this is going on, the body color is changing from one color pattern to another color pattern attracting fish from a distance, especially in clear water. Other good jerkbaits include the Rapala Husky Jerk and the Lucky Craft Jerk bait.

Tubes are also deadly on staging smallmouth both on their initial migration out of deep water or after they backpedal after a cold front. Smallmouth will hit a tube regardless of the weather conditions. Drag the tube across the bottom with an occasional pause. If you have short strikes and can't set the hook on a smallmouth try downsizing your tube. Another favorite tactic of mine is to cut the tentacles of the tube in half. This will shorten the overall length of the tube, bringing the end of the tube closer to the hook and increase the number of hooked smallmouth.

The old reliable Wacky Worm rig will catch smallmouth under just about any situation and an early season cold front is no exception. My favorite spring Wacky Worm rig is a four inch Case magic Stick with a number 2 Kahle hook under a red O ring. By using the Case O-Wacky Tool to place the O ring on the worm the angler will cut down considerably on the number of worms that are used in a day of fishing.

When fishing a Wacky Worm I will leave some slack in the line and watch for any movement. If you have a tight line, a sluggish pre-spawn smallmouth can sense the slightest resistance and drop the bait. When watching your line, remember that even the slightest movement is probably a pick up. When you see line movement, drop your rod tip and slowly reel up the slack. Set the hook with an upward sweep and don't try to cross the smallmouth's eyes. Too fast a hookset will result in a missed fish.

Bob Dekker with a *Wacky Worm* pre-spawn smallmouth

Your choice in line will decide how many fish you will put in the boat. Although popular with many anglers, braided line is not the best choice. Braided line does not sink as fast as fluorocarbon or monofilament line and since you do not want to weight your Wacky Worm, you won't get down to the desired depth, especially if you have any current. Monofilament line is a good choice since it will sink, and the stretch in the line can help an angler who sets the hook too fast. The ideal line is a Hybrid fluorocarbon/monofilament line. The fluorocarbon sinks with the slightest amount of weight making it ideal for finicky pre-spawn smallmouth. Many of these hybrid lines are specially designed for a spinning reel. Trust me, hybrid line will out fish braided line while Wacky Worm fishing by at least 3 to 1.

Along with your choice of line, your choice of rod is also critical. The ideal rod is a six foot six or seven foot rod with a moderately fast action but with enough power to handle a 20 inch smallmouth. If your rod is too light, you won't get a good hookset. *My preferred rod is a Smallmouth Series Plus 6'6" medium light action rod with a fast tip for finesse presentations. This rod is ideal for finesse presentations when fishing four to six pound test fluorocarbon or monofilament line. When fishing with light line I prefer to use a spinning rod as opposed to a casting rod.*

Transition areas can be prime staging areas for big pre-spawn females. As water temperatures rise during the day females will start to roam the shallows and continue doing so until the sun starts to wane, causing the water temperature to reverse its procedure. Once the water temperature drops only a few degrees the female smallmouth begin to move. As they move out of the shallows they will often stack up along the first transition from soft to hard bottom and on many reservoirs this is usually a steep rock shoreline.

Big smallmouth will hold tightly to the steep rock transitions overnight and remain there the next day until the water temperature repeats it procedure. Even if the transition is not present smallmouth will use steep rock banks as migration routes from deep to shallow water. Most anglers will launch their boat and head into the shallows and pass up the honey hole. The smart angler will stop at the transition, cast a suspending jerkbait, soft plastic jerkbait, grub, jig and minnow or a crankbait and start the day with a few big smallmouth.

Don't make the mistake of passing up the transition in the morning and heading for the shallows. You might catch a few small males while fishing the shallows and you might even have some fun, but if the water temperature drops overnight the big fish will not be there. If you wait to fish the transition until late morning you will also find a lack of big fish. As the day progresses and the water temperature rises a few degrees the temperature will trigger smallmouth to head back towards the shallows. This might not be a quick movement and the fish will spread out and be tough to locate, making for tough fishing.

By late afternoon smallmouth will be back suspending off the edge of the transition and be very catchable. In fact, the first time I caught big smallmouth relating to a transition was in the afternoon when the bite in the shallows had stopped. I had about an hour left on a guide trip and decided to give a steep rocky shoreline a try even though I had fished it several times before during the day with little if any success. I had my client cast a crankbait, hoping to kill some time before heading back to the boat landing and then bang, after the third cast he connected with a 20 incher, which was the big smallmouth of the day. No, I did not keep the big fish for last even though my client might have thought that.

At first I did not dwell on this, thinking that my client had managed to stumble into a gift fish. I had the guy booked for the next day and how could

Fishing For Smallmouth Bass

we not make the place where he caught the big fish the day before our first stop. I was hoping that there would be at least one big smallmouth but to my surprise my client boated 5 smallmouth in the 20 inch class. I even got into the act and caught a 20 incher with a grub. Since that time that transition along with a few others are a regular morning and afternoon stop on my guide trips.

When the water temperature climbs into the upper 50 or low 60 degree range smallmouth enter the late pre-spawn period. At that time plastics and jerkbaits remain effective but topwater baits become effective. While fishing with a topwater bait is never a guarantee the closer that smallmouth are to spawning the more predictable the topwater bite is. The topwater bite can be sporadic and you will need to make adjustments.

One May I had a client that missed several giant smallmouth and both he and I were getting frustrated. I was fishing the used water with a Case Magic Stick rigged wacky style and hooking my client's missed smallmouth. Although I was catching smallmouth my client was getting strikes on the Hubs Chub and he was content to keep using the bait. I knew that it was not the Hubs Chub that was missing smallmouth but the overzealous client. This is a common dilemma for a fishing guide.

I approached the situation with caution and suggested to him that he needed to slow down the bait. Seeing that my client was not responding to my coaching it was time for an attitude adjustment. As we approached a downed tree that is a steady producer of big smallmouth, I positioned the boat in a way that it would be next to impossible for my client to get a good cast at the tree. I quickly grabbed another rod, and pitched a bone/shad Hubs Chub tight to a downed tree at the edge of a creek channel. I let the Hubs Chub settle, reeled up the slack and raised my rod about a foot. This caused the Hubs Chub to emit a slight pop. All at once the water exploded and we both watched a 21 inch smallmouth fly out of the water. My client was mesmerized and did not realize he had been bamboozled. He asked, "How did you do that?" I eagerly replied, "I finessed the bait."

I told my client, "Watch carefully what I do on my next cast." I made another cast at the same downed tree, let the Hubs Cub settle, raised my rod again and hooked another big smallmouth. After the smallmouth was released I handed my client the rod and he repeated my technique. He did not get a strike on that cast, but he continued finessing the bait and eventually hooked a 19 inch smallmouth. The rest of the day he caught 14 smallmouth and only missed three. I explained to my client that the Hubs Chub drops vertically in the water and the BB's in the lure cause it to quiver.

An active smallmouth will often hammer the Hubs Chub but a neutral smallmouth will be attracted to the quivering and suck in the bait and slowly pull it under. There is no way to know how a smallmouth will react to the bait so the angler needs to be prepared the second the bait hits the water. Popping baits that drop vertically in the water can also work under this situation.

Spring cold fronts can give pre-spawn smallmouth lock-jaw and push them tight to wood cover. While a topwater bait might not be my first choice under cold front conditions, if there is not too much wind they will catch big smallmouth. I look for big smallmouth to hold tight to wood cover adjacent to spawning areas. I will cast my Hubs Chub tight to the wood cover without throwing the bait into the wood. If the bait hits the wood and gets hung up, it's all over. Once the surface bait lands next to the wood, let it settle and give a fast pop and then let it sit and finesse the bait. The fast pop will get the smallmouth's attention and a slight twitch will trigger a strike. Try twitching the bait two or three times, quickly retrieve the surface bait and then repeat the presentation.

Natural Lakes

Natural lakes will take longer to warm but the water temperature will hold constant and not drop as severely overnight. When the water warms to about 45 degrees the pre-spawn bite can be phenomenal.

The early pre-spawn bite can be tough. Following ice out, locating and catching smallmouth can be difficult on many clear lakes. The deeper the lake the slower it warms and the longer smallmouth hold in their wintering areas. Wintering areas are typically deep rock humps, the deep edge of points, deep wood and fish cribs. These deep smallmouth can be tough to locate even with good electronics since they hold very tight to cover. Even when you do locate them they can be tough to catch.

I have found the most aggressive smallmouth to be those relating to fish cribs. Fish cribs are common on many northern lakes and are usually put in lakes with limited or no natural structure. Most fish cribs have been permanent fixtures in lakes for many years and the longer they have been in the lake the more inviting they are to smallmouth bass. As a fish crib ages it begins to deteriorate and it becomes more fertile attracting a variety of organisms and fish.

Fish cribs are a popular haunt of panfisherman but bassers often pass them up, especially in spring. Smallmouth winter on the deep edges of fish cribs and, unlike natural structure, they tend to be more aggressive. The problem is that these fish crib related smallmouth won't rise up in the water column to strike a bait until the water temperature rises into the mid 40 degree range. You will need to use your electronics and position your boat over the fish and vertical jig with either a hair jig or a lead head jig tipped with a minnow. I have experimented with drop shot rigs and caught a few smallmouth but I always catch more fish with jigs. Once the water warms up, drop shot rigs can out fish jigs. Before smallmouth abandon the cribs as they enter into the pre-spawn they will rise up into the water column to strike a bait. At this time both lipless crankbaits and suspending jerkbaits become very productive.

Once the water temperature climbs to the mid forty degree range smallmouth begin to move out of the deep structure and move into pre-spawn staging areas. Barring a severe cold front they will remain in close proximity of these staging areas and are usually easy to locate. The advantage to staging smallmouth on clear lakes is that they will stack up in larger schools than in stained water reservoirs. Pre-spawn smallmouth will also suspend more in clear water lakes as opposed to stained water which makes them all the easier to locate.

One word of caution, when dealing with water temperature on deep clear lakes you don't always get what you see. Water temperatures can warm very slowly. Your locator might read 45 degrees on the surface but it is much colder on the edge of the deep hole where smallmouth are holding. As far as smallmouth are concerned it is still winter and they have no reason to leave their deep water sanctuary.

Just as on a stained water reservoir, steep rock structure is a prime staging area. If you are looking for the honey hole look for a transition. The transition can be rock/sand, rock/gravel, or rock/soft bottom. After any weather change or slight drop in water temperature these transitions can be a magnet. What happens is the water temperature surrounding the rock shoreline will be a few degrees cooler. It is the transition in the water temperature that attracts the smallmouth and not the physical transition. Trust me, these smallmouth are very catchable and you can have a fantastic time.

Fishing clear water always dictates using caution and taking extra precautions during the pre-spawn will mean more and bigger smallmouth. If you move in too fast you will spook the big smallmouth and, while you might catch a few fish, the school will scatter. I will stop my outboard far short of the transition. Besides not spooking the big smallmouth it gives me a chance to fish the open water adjacent form the transition. Start fishing the open water with either a lipless crankbait or a swim bait. After I catch a few smallmouth on either the swim bait or lipless crankbait and the action slows, I switch to a suspending jerkbait.

If you are looking to catch big smallmouth from clear water lakes during the pre-spawn, plan on using suspending jerkbaits. This jerkbait pattern holds true whether you are fishing a 1,000 acre lake or the Great Lakes. For jerkbaits to be effective the angler needs to adapt his presentation to the mood of the smallmouth. Since fishing with suspending jerkbaits in the cold spring water can require intense concentration and persistence this pattern is not for the overzealous angler.

The average angler will typically work a jerkbait with a sharp tug, let the jerkbait suspend and after a few seconds follow up with another sharp tug. If the water temperature is on the rise and smallmouth are aggressive this technique works great. Cool water temperatures and post-frontal conditions which are typical during the pre-spawn call for a very slow approach.

I have found the most productive method is to dead-stick the jerk bait. After you cautiously position your boat, make a long cast to the general area of the transition. Next crank the jerkbait down to its maximum depth with 10 to 15 turns of the reel handle. Stop reeling, letting the jerkbait "dead-stick" or sit absolutely motionless in a suspending mode. The trick is in deciding how long to let the jerkbait sit motionless. On average I let the jerkbait suspend for at least two minutes. If I am sure smallmouth are present I will let the jerkbait suspend for as long as five minutes. As the jerkbait is suspending motionless, make sure there is sufficient slack in your line to compensate for boat movement, especially if there is a chop on the water. It is important to watch the slack line for any movement. Even the slightest movement of the line in one direction or the other can mean a smallmouth has taken the jerkbait. If you do want to move the jerkbait a bit do so by moving the rod tip and not the reel. You don't want to jerk the bait but slowly rock it.

Dead sticking a jerkbait is not something I do on a typical pre-spawn guide trip. Not that I am trying to hold something back from my clients, but if I was to try and share this presentation most of them would think I was trying to kill some time because I knew that the fish had lockjaw. All I can say is that this is the most deadly presentation I have ever encountered for catching big pre-spawn smallmouth when fishing under post frontal conditions.

Fishing For Smallmouth Bass

Suspending jerkbaits are great for catching giant pre-spawn smallmouth but they are not a very good search bait. For locating active pre-spawn smallmouth it is tough to beat a lipless crankbait. Lipless crankbaits are very versatile, they can be fished shallow or deep, fast or slow. You can use a steady or stop-n-go retrieve. These baits have a fast sink rate so count down to the desired depth when fishing deeper water. Make long casts parallel to deep sloped banks. It is important to keep the lipless crankbait in the strike zone as long as possible.

I prefer 1/4 to 1/2 ounce lipless crankbaits and use a six foot six medium action spinning rod. My spinning reel is spooled with either eight pound fluorocarbon or monofilament line. It is important to tie directly to the split ring to produce better action. The only modification I make is to replace the front hook with a red treble hook. This tends to produce more strikes at the center of the bait for better hook ups.

Just as when fishing a stained water reservoir, soft plastics will also do the job on clear lakes. The presentation is basically the same although you will have to experiment with colors. For wacky worming my favorite colors are watermelon, green pumpkin, junebug and black. The preferred color can change at any time so make sure you hit the water with a good selection. When using soft plastic jerkbaits white and green pumpkin work best.

Rivers

Locating pre-spawn smallmouth can be tough to pattern and can often be a mystery for anglers. On reservoirs and natural lakes there is little change from one year to the next. Once an angler learns a specific body of water they can return annually to connect with smallmouth. With a river, no two years are exactly the same. You might have had great fishing on your spring outing the previous year but when you return the following year and fish the same areas you may end up without a strike.

River smallmouth do not stack in the huge numbers during the pre-spawn like they do in natural lakes and reservoirs. Although you can find pockets of several smallmouth you will need to keep on the move and not spend a great deal of time in any one area even if you caught a few big smallmouth. Instead of dwelling on a hotspot you will do yourself a favor by returning to a spot several times throughout the day.

The first place to look for pre-spawn river smallmouth is any slack water area. During low water smallmouth will fan out across slack water.

Crankbaits can easily be worked over this open water and will quickly let the angler know if smallmouth are present.

If the water is high in spring, look for most smallmouth to be holding tight to the shoreline. I like to cast a soft plastic minnow imitation jerkbait or a spinnerbait tight to the shoreline and wood cover. If the cover is not too dense shallow running crankbaits and suspending jerkbaits can be effective. Stick baits rigged wacky style and tubes will also be hot baits at times.

High water pushes smallmouth tight to the shoreline

The most consistent areas are backwaters or sloughs with rock, gravel or sand. These hard bottom areas void of heavy current are one of the few places where large concentrations of smallmouth can be found. Actual smallmouth location will depend on the flow of the river. The higher the water and swifter the flow the further smallmouth will be pushed into the slough. While they won't spawn on soft bottom they will seek out sand.

Fishing For Smallmouth Bass

Fishing can also be fantastic during the pre-spawn on a river. One such fantastic day was the late May day I spent fishing with Joe Nieciak and his son Matt. I knew that the smallmouth would still be in their staging which was on the edge of a small slough. I knew fishing could be tough since the smallmouth were preparing to spawn, and I also knew that the funky weather pattern we were in would have an effect on the bite. Since Joe was bringing along his son the main objective was to make the outing special for the young angler. This would mean I would need to simplify my presentation.

I picked up Joe and Matt at Popps Resort and had them pick up four dozen jumbo leeches at the bait shop, then we headed for the Menominee River to catch a bunch of smallmouth. We talked a bit about the incoming nasty weather, but I assured them that my prediction was that we would stay dry most of the day. It does pay to have a positive attitude when dealing with the weather even though it is out of your control.

After launching my boat I opted to go right to the honey hole knowing the weather was up in the air and it was important to start catching fish from the get go. I rigged both Joe and Matt with four inch Case Magic Sticks rigged wacky style. After a few casts to get the feel of the wacky worm my clients began catching smallmouth. The good bite continued until the south wind shifted and sputtered out of the east. I could see that Joe and Matt were getting light bites but the hook ups were non-existent.

I told my clients that it was time to change baits. I tied on number four red octopus hooks, placed a BB sized split shot about a foot up from the hook and dressed the hook with a Jumbo leech. On the first cast, BINGO! Matt connected with a nice smallmouth. I told Joe that when the wind shifts to the east and the barometric pressure changes, nothing is more effective than a leech on a hook. Even though the bite remained light, unlike plastics, a live leech is something a spring smallmouth can't resist.

We did have to cut the day a bit short because the front eventually moved our way. I checked my phone for an updated radar and just to the west I saw plenty of yellow and orange headed our way. I showed it to Joe and he agreed that we should head back to the boat landing. The only complaint was from Matt who insisted that we had rain coats and a little rain was not going to harm us. While it is great to see a kid so fired up about fishing, common sense ruled. Shortly after the boat was on the trailer it started to rain buckets, not to mention the thunder boomers. It was a great day as Joe and Matt caught over 30 dandy smallmouth.

Fishing for pre-spawn smallmouth need not be a time of confusion as long as the angler understands the conditions and how smallmouth relate to them. Simply put, you need to learn to deal with the changing weather and moody smallmouth.

Fishing For Smallmouth Bass

Mark Follett with a with a pre spawn smallmouth that was holding on a transition area

Pre-spawn is big fish time!

Pre-spawn reservoir smallmouth

Chapter 5
The Spawn

Few anglers pay much attention to what happens during the spawn and how vulnerable smallmouth are. Being a member of the sunfish family, the chores of building and protecting the nest are a job of the male. Male smallmouth will both build nests and use existing rock and rubble, or a combination of both. The nests can be in water as shallow as two feet in dark water and as deep as 20 feet in clear water. When constructing the nest the male will use his caudal fin to vigorously form a circular ridge on the edge of the nest. At this time he will also move any foreign objects from the nest. Construction of the nest can take as long as 48 hours depending on the type of bottom. Nest size will depend on the size of the male, and will generally be twice his length. The finished nest will be from 18 to 36 inches.

Actual spawning will not necessarily take place right after nest completion but only when the desired water temperature is reached which is between 60 -70 degrees. At this time the female will leave deep water. During the actual spawn there is a great transformation in the female. Her color becomes pale, almost white but the markings are very noticeable. The pair will remain on the nest anywhere from one to three hours. There are a series of emissions with 25 to 60 eggs being deposited at 30 second intervals. If the male is still ripe, he will attract another female onto the nest. The female will also search out another male if she has eggs left. This is a very crucial time and should never be interrupted. Even though neither the male or female will strike baits at this time, any interruption would be disastrous.

Spawn

After spawning, the male takes the job of guarding the nest. Unfortunately, they are easily caught by even novice anglers. The male smallmouth will savagely attack a bait as it protects the nest as opposed to striking the bait. If the male is taken off the nest, the eggs or fry will become a feast for panfish or predator fish.

Many bass anglers insist that it is unethical to fish for bedded bass. That being said, in most waters that would mean abstaining from fishing for bass for 2-3 weeks. After studying smallmouth for over 30 years I have concluded that fishing for bedded bass is acceptable if the proper restraints are taken. Being a full time fishing guide I can't afford to take a vacation not to mention that my client are interested in catching fish.

First off anglers should avoid using ultra light tackle during the spawn. Light tackle may seem sporting with the smallmouth but should not be used when fishing during the spawn. Light tackle will command a long fight which will only add more anxiety in this time of extreme tension. Even if a smallmouth is released immediately a stressed out male will migrate slowly back to the nest and the damage can detrimental by the time it eventually returns to the nest.

Anglers should use soft plastics as much as possible. The biggest bonus to fishing with soft plastics is you only use a single barbless hook which will make for an easy release and less likely to damage the fish. If the bite is light as it usually is during the spawn it is important to give the bait too much time before setting the hook. This will result in the smallmouth swallowing the hook which can mean an end to the smallmouth and the fry on the nest. If this is a persistent problem than make sure you clinch down the barbs on the hook.

Topwater fishing can be very effective and on some days the only way to consistently catch these tenacious opponents. However most topwater baits have treble hooks and again anglers need to use caution and release the fish as quickly as possible back into the water. Also anglers should pinch the barbs on their hooks.

Yes, you can fish for smallmouth during the spawn as long as you use retrain along with some common sense. Release the smallmouth back into the water ASAP.

Chapter 6
Post Spawn

During the post-spawn period I have experienced both good and bad fishing. It may not be a prime time to catch big smallmouth but you can find active smallmouth and have a productive day. It is indeed a challenge and, except for a major cold front or a severe change in water levels, a persistent angler should be able to catch fish. Being a guide out on the water on a daily basis, my opinion is that you cannot use the post-spawn as an excuse for tough fishing.

Each body of water is different and that can complicate fishing. Over the years I have observed that if smallmouth spawn early or late in one body of water that this is an annual event. So once you establish early and late spawning on a particular body of water you can fish it accordingly. Smallmouth on one lake may be aggressive while on a lake a few miles away with the same water temperature smallmouth can be inactive.

Water temperature is also the key to catching post-spawn smallmouth. If water temperatures are on the rise smallmouth will be aggressive and cooperate. However, if water temperatures drop after spawning, fishing can be very tough. So first off, you need to look for the warmest possible water temperatures and choose water where fluctuating water temperatures are less common.

Plastics are my first choice when fishing for post-spawn smallmouth and while I use grubs, tubes, stick baits and jerkbaits, I match my plastics with the depth and conditions. For example, if I am fishing a river or stained water reservoir I use tubes, skirted grubs, grubs and stick baits. Smallmouth will be holding tight to wood or rocks and both the tube and wacky worm can be fished tight to the cover. The secret is to work the baits as slowly and as tight to cover as possible. Another option would be to finesse a topwater bait around the cover.

Skirted grubs can be an excellent choice when smallmouth are in the post-spawn. This can be a difficult time for a guide particularly when his clients are hoping to catch big fish. On one tough guide trip I was having trouble locating smallmouth and it finally dawned on me that maybe the smallmouth were holding in the stumps. The stump field was about sixty feet out from the shore and ran parallel to the shoreline. I had caught smallmouth in the stumps before and it was time to make a move. The other thought that entered my mind was that even if we did not catch smallmouth there might be a few largemouth bass swimming in the stumps that would supply action for my clients. Fish were fish and a guide has to do what he can so the clients can have some fun. So I turned the boat around and headed for the stumps.

Fishing For Smallmouth Bass

I gave one of my clients a single tail skirted grub rigged on a wide gap hook with a bullet weight and the other client a shallow running crankbait. I told the client that I chose a single tail grub due to the post-spawn. I added that if we were fishing this wood under stable weather and warming water temperatures I would have chosen a twin tailed skirted grub.

The client with the shallow running crankbait struck first before his partner had a chance to make a cast. He made a cast tight to a stump, twitched it and the water exploded. I hoped it was a big bass but I was skeptical due to the size of the splash when the fish hit the bait. My client had either tied into a state record bass or a northern pike. Regrettably, my inclinations were right and once I saw the length of the fish and the tail, I knew it was no bass. It was a big northern pike, and now the problem was to get the pike into the boat before the pike bit the line and ate my $10 crankbait! Well, the pike won the battle and as my client reeled in his slack line he asked, "You got any more of those crankbaits."

Now, while I had a few more in my tackle box, I told him that was the last one and he gave me a funny look as I handed him a skirted grub. After all, I knew that if I gave the guy another crankbait he would cast it tight to another stump, twitch it, and probably hook another pike and lose another $10 crankbait. If he would have lost his crankbait and not mine I am sure he would not have tied on another one. Some clients just have no respect for the guide's tackle.

I told my clients to aim for the stumps, let the skirted grub fall and when they had slack line to give the grub a short hop and drag it slowly back to the boat. What I stressed most was to let the skirted grub drop and that when they felt a strike to count to two before setting the hook. They made several casts without a pick up and the guy who lost the pike to a crankbait said, "I think we should be throwing crankbaits, they want a fast retrieve."

I was just getting ready to politely tell my client that we were after bass and not pike when his partner set the hook on what I thought was a big largemouth bass. This time I was glad it was not a largemouth bass as the fish turned out to be a 20 inch smallmouth bass. The smallmouth was big and before spawning would have easily pushed 5 pounds. After my client took a few photos the smallmouth was released back into the water and headed right back to the stump. I was hoping that we had developed a pattern.

The bite was slow, which is typical during the post-spawn, but the good news was that we caught smallmouth and they were big. It took a while for my clients to grasp the concept of fishing slow, especially the guy that insisted on throwing a crankbait. It was actually quite simple: if they retrieved the skirted grub too fast or were too quick with the hook set they would not catch any fish. This was one of those days when doing everything just right was the difference between a bad and good day on the water.

One of the misconceptions about the post-spawn is that smallmouth head for deep water immediately after spawning. While some females do indeed head for deep water many remain shallow, particularly in reservoirs where wood is present. If smallmouth are holding tight to the bottom or tight to wood cover a stick bait is a deadly lure if you use the proper presentation.

In order for the stick bait to be effective you will need to drag it along the bottom. This will take patience since a 20 inch post-spawn smallmouth can bite like a small perch. Mix in a cold front and a drop in water temperature and you can expect the bite to be light. Since I don't like to add weight to a stick bait if at all possible, this technique works best in water less than six feet deep. I don't worry about wind since I try to avoid wind when fishing for pre-spawn smallmouth. Areas out of the wind and in direct sunlight see warmer water temperatures.

When dragging the stick bait across the bottom it is critical to pause occasionally. About 80 percent of your strikes will occur on the pause. Just as with working the bait higher in the water column, the movement will get the smallmouth's attention. If the bite is light I will drag the stick bait about two feet and let it sit for as long as one minute. If the bite is more aggressive I will pause my retrieve about five or ten seconds. On many days one definite pattern is the longer the pause the larger the smallmouth.

On another one of those intolerable weather days I had two old codgers fishing with me. They had fished with me several times in the past during the summer and fall. I told them that the fishing could be great but that in May inclement weather could put a damper on the fishing, unlike fall when a cold front can put big smallmouth on the feed bag. So instead of partaking in the pre spawn bite they booked a trip in mid June and we were faced with the post-spawn.

They were familiar with stick baits since they had used them while fishing with me in summer. Before we got started I showed them how we would be hooking them Texas style with a 4/0 wide gap hook instead of wacky style like in the summer. I knew where the smallmouth were holding so even with the cold front we would not have to search for them, although I was hoping that they were not holding too tight to the bottom. Not that they are not catchable when they are holding tight to the bottom, but for anglers with marginal fishing ability it can make for tough fishing.

We tried fishing the stick baits higher in the water column but could not even get a strike. Finally, I decided to head for a favorite stump field that always held smallmouth during tough conditions. My clients made perfect casts, dropping the stick baits tight to the stumps. However, even though I kept stressing that they retrieve the bait slowly and give a long pause it was not registering. It didn't take long for me to realize that this was not going to work.

I was thinking of what I could do next when I watched one of my clients trying to untangle a birds' nest. After I heard a few not so nice words he nicely mentioned that I needed to put new line on his reel. I didn't say a word and just watched as he messed around with the line for three or four minutes before he untangled his mess. I am too nice of a guy to tell him that I had just re-spooled his reel the night before and that it was operator error! Finally, he reeled up the slack and yelled, "I got one!
Soon after his bone shaking yell I landed a 21 inch female smallmouth.

The worst part about the whole thing is I could not get him to comprehend that the big smallmouth hit the stick bait because it was sitting motionlessly on the bottom. He thought that it hit the stick bait on his retrieve and he said that when he reeled in the slack he pulled the bass out of the stump.

On the next cast he went back to the fast retrieve and he went back to catching no bass. After a while, I became frustrated because I knew the smallmouth were present and I could not get my clients to slow down their retrieve. I was actually hoping for him to get a birds' nest so a smallmouth might pick up the stick bait lying on the bottom, even if it meant that I would have to respool the reel again. I did manage to salvage the day by putting the stick baits away and having my client fish with leeches on a slip bobber. If that technique does not work you might as well put the boat on the trailer.

If you are dealing with wind or smallmouth are holding in water deeper than six feet you will need to add weight to the stick bait. Weighted wide gap hooks will work but if the bite is light the added weight might cause a smallmouth to refuse your offering. If the wood cover is not too overwhelming I will use a finesse rig. My post-spawn finesse rig is what many anglers refer to as the Mojo-Rig. The original Mojo Slip Shot fishing sinker is designed to drag the weight over the bottom and through deep grass. The long cylindrical design of the Slip Shot has less points to catch grass and cover while fishing and it can be easily positioned and secured anywhere ahead of the bait. This rig will allow the stick bait to drop but not cause the weight to have too much resistance for a persnickety post-spawn smallmouth.

Rigging up a Mojo Rig is easy. All you need to do is slide on a sinker and tie on a 1/0 wide gap hook and peg the weight to the line. The rubber pegs made by the Mojo Tackle Company work fine but they are expensive so I will use a toothpick to peg the Mojo sinker onto the line. Next, select your bait of choice and slide the pegged weight up the line to whatever leader size you desire. There are a number of plastics that can be used with the Mojo rig when working deep sand grass for smallmouth bass. I prefer to use cylindrical jerkbaits like Yamamoto Senkos and Case Magic Sticks, four and six inch finesse worms and lizards. When working wood, or any other cover for that matter, it is important to Texas rig your plastics. If you are fishing an unobstructed bottom you can use an octopus hook. This finesse rig can be frustrating to use since you will get the weight hung up. However, it is very effective.

Dealing with post-spawn smallmouth in clear water lakes can be a bit more challenging than when fishing in a river or reservoir. Just as in a shallow reservoir, smallmouth will move tight to cover, but oftentimes cover close to a spawning area is usually sparse.

The first place I search for post-spawn smallmouth is a transition from hard to soft bottom along the shoreline. I have observed spawned out females cruising along the shorelines and once they move into a transition area they will stop their horizontal movement and start dropping down into the water column following the transition. Some smallmouth will descend tight to the bottom while others will suspend. They continue to follow the transition until they encounter cover which can be downed wood, rubble or boulders. Even the slightest amount of cover can attract several smallmouth.

My favorite presentation for dealing with post-spawn smallmouth relating to a transition is a grub. When fishing a grub I am able to fish throughout the water column until I connect with active smallmouth. I start out casting a grub parallel to the shoreline to catch any smallmouth that are suspending. Suspending post-spawn smallmouth may not be overly aggressive but they will hit a properly placed grub. The problem is that they will not rise too far to chase the grub so you will need to retrieve the grub at different depths with each cast. Once you enter the strike zone continue to work that depth until the action stops.

Next, I cast tight to the shoreline and retrieve the grub a few feet under the surface. Just like when I was casting parallel to the shoreline I let my grub drop to a different depth on each cast until I find the strike zone. If I am not getting any response swimming the grub across the water column I will occasionally lift my rod and then drop it a few feet allowing the grub to flutter in the water column. I wait a few seconds and continue my retrieve. This will trigger a strike from smallmouth following the grub. Before you start your retrieve make sure you are in control of your rod since strikes can be fast and hard.

I use a variety of grubs but my favorite for post-spawn smallmouth is the Zipper grub, but I also use three and four inch curly tail grubs. I rig the grub and a darter head jig with a quality hook. The longer hook shank on the darter head jig gives the jig a more horizontal profile. This horizontal profile is critical in the action of the grub. The long shank will place the hook closer to the rear of the grub allowing for a better hookset. When you feel a strike, stop your retrieve, count to two or three and set the hook. A post-spawn smallmouth might sit on the grub for a few seconds and if you set the hook too quickly you will miss the fish. Once a post-spawn smallmouth refuses a bait they usually end up with lockjaw.

Color can make a difference so plan on experimenting. My favorite colors are green pumpkin, watermelon, black and blue. I use both single colored and bi-colored grubs and occasionally use grubs with silver or gold flakes. Again, it is important to be creative since there is nothing cut in stone.

On many natural lakes prime spawning occurs on points. After spawning is complete, smallmouth remain on the point but catching them can be tough. If you are fishing during a stable weather pattern post -spawn smallmouth male smallmouth will go on the feed. Unfortunately, it will take time along with stable weather to motivate the larger females. As I mentioned previously, the deeper a post-spawn female drops into the water column the tougher they are to catch. If they are suspending at random depths throughout the water column they definitely have the "post-spawn blues" and you might have more luck playing the lottery.

When smallmouth are holding off the deep edge of a point it's hard to beat a drop shot rig. A drop shot rig will allow the angler to keep the bait on the bottom and right in front of the mouth of a smallmouth. This is imperative when smallmouth suspend off the deep edge of a point and feed on small perch. If that is the case you will need to modify your rig. Instead of the typical 14-18 inch tag line out from the palomar knot, I use a four to six inch tag line. Perch are bottom feeders so it is important to

81

keep your bait close to the bottom. Along with the short tag line I tie on a 1/0 wide gap hook and Texas rig a three inch perch imitation soft plastic minnow bait. If you get light bites and can't hook any smallmouth, switch to a standard drop shot hook and nose hook the minnow.

Most anglers prefer a 6'6" medium power rod with a fast tip for fishing with drop shot rigs. My Smallmouth Series Plus SPS66ML rod has performed great for using drop shot presentations. Even if you have the right rod you need to perform the right hookset. I prefer the "reel set" to set the hook rather than the traditional "rip the lips" hookset. The sharp light wire drop shot hooks will penetrate easily with light pressure and you risk breaking the light line on a heavy bass with a hard hookset. A 'reel set" just means you reel in line as you lift the rod, all in one motion creating a steadily increasing pressure on the point of the hook instead of quick, sharp, line snapping jerks. If you buy cheap equipment you will be sorry since you will probably end up with a broken rod.

After spawning is complete river smallmouth can remain in the shallows as long as crayfish are present. Male smallmouth will be aggressive after they leave the nest and a wacky worm is the ideal presentation. Since these male smallmouth are aggressive they will grab the stick bait without hesitation, often moving it quickly to keep it from another male smallmouth. It is necessary to be prepared for strikes as soon as the bait hits the water. Watch for slack line, because it is common for a smallmouth to pick up the stick bait and head for deep water which means diving towards the boat. It is critical to reel in all the slack line before setting the hook, otherwise the smallmouth can drop the bait.

The only problem with rigging a stick bait wacky style is that they are a one fish bait. By hooking the worm through the center you weaken it. By the time you grab your catch all you have is the hook as the two pieces of stick bait fall into the water. In fact, the first year I was using senkos I was more concerned about saving the bait instead of getting the bass in the boat. These baits were too hard to come by to watch them fall to the bottom of the river. On more than one day we ran out of the hot color and that was almost enough to make a grown man cry.

I quickly learned that while these baits are effective they are also expensive and since I was using them on a daily basis I had to figure out something other than a surcharge for my clients. Well, I did not figure it out myself but one winter I was at a sport show when a tournament fishermen showed me how to place an O ring on a wacky worm. I went out and bought a bunch of O-rings and saved a ton of money the following year.

Fishing For Smallmouth Bass

Shortly after that I started using the O-Wacky Tool produced by Case plastics. The tool goes over the worm and allows you to push the O ring onto the center of the worm with ease. This tool allows for the use of a slightly smaller O-ring than you can put on by hand. If the O ring is too loose it will defeat the purpose since you will need to skin hook the stick bait allowing it to break in half when you catch a fish. Case Plastics also makes a complete line of stick baits called Magic Stiks.

Another advantage to using an O-ring is that I believe it increases your hooking percentage. With the hook more exposed on the hook set, the odds are higher that the hook will find the smallmouth's mouth. I have no statistics to back that other than just by observing the increased catch of my clients. My clients have a wide range of differing levels of expertise and I believe that a more exposed hook has helped them all regardless of their ability .

A cold front that coincides with the post-spawn can give smallmouth lockjaw. Under these conditions a tube dragged along the transition can salvage the day. On one wretched day my clients had about had it with the 30 mph northwest winds and intermittent rain showers. We hit the river in the morning and while the conditions were not great I did not feel there was need to panic. Yes, we were dealing with a cold front but I told my clients that river smallmouth are generally more resilient than their cousins in lakes and reservoirs.

At mid day we only had two sub legal smallmouth with both the water and air temperature plunging. I did not know if the befuddled looks on my clients' faces were due to the weather or if they were about ready to strangle me, thinking that I had known all along that the fish weren't going to bite and was just taking them for a boat ride. At least I knew they would not throw me overboard since they didn't have a clue where they were. As the wind increased all three of us contemplated heading back to the boat landing.

I told my clients that there was one more spot that we had to try and neither one of my clients gave me a response. I put my trolling motor on high speed and cruised the shoreline looking for the transition in a last ditch effort to locate a few smallmouth. Once I hit the transition I adjusted my electronics to maximum sensitivity. As I expected, things continued to look

Cold Front Smallmouth

for the worse since I did not see one fish on the screen. Easing the boat out to deeper water the boat moved over a large submerged log and I noticed a few good sized arcs just above the log. I yelled to my clients, "Look there *are* fish in this river!" and pointed to the arcs on the screen.

Knowing that it was impossible to hold the boat over the fish with my trolling motor I made a sharp 90 degree turn, headed upstream a bit and carefully dropped the anchor. I tightened up the slack in the anchor rope as the boat was positioned parallel to the shoreline about ten feet deeper than where we marked the fish.

Both my clients were already using tubes but I told them that we would need to retie and switch from the jigheads to wide gap hooks and bullet weights so we could rig the tubes weedless. They quickly responded this time and I could see a spark in both their eyes. I just hoped we could catch a few fish.

After they retied I instructed them to cast towards the shoreline and to slowly drag the tube along the bottom. On his first cast my client said, "I am stuck in the wood!" A few seconds later he yelled, "Fish On!"

As I scooped an 18" smallmouth into the net, I explained to my client that the smallmouth was holding on the edge of the wood and that he had probably bumped the wood with the tube, triggering the strike. Both my clients managed to catch a few nice smallmouth before the well went dry.

It was by no means a banner day, but the lesson learned was, don't give up and when everything else fails, drag a tube. The only presentation that will out fish a tube under these harsh conditions is a live minnow or leech fished on either a jighead or a plain hook. So, if you are dealt with this disaster, swallow your pride and bring some live bait along.

Another place I search for post-spawn smallmouth is the first distinct breakline out from a spawning area. Instead of cruising the shoreline, other smallmouth, particularly on natural lakes, will drop vertically in the water column after spawning. As they ascend they will hold tightly on any abrupt change along the bottom. These fish can be from 8 to 20 feet or anywhere in between and are easily marked with good electronics. Just as when fishing along a transition, look for downed wood to be a fish magnet. In clear water smallmouth tend to suspend more than in a river or stained water reservoir.

During stable weather patterns casting lipless crankbaits parallel to the breakline is an effective pattern. The faster you can get the lipless crankbait down to the desired depth and keep it in the strike zone the more smallmouth you will hook. Along with crankbaits, grubs and finesse jigs are another option.

A cold front will push smallmouth tight to the bottom and since they are recovering from the stress of spawning they are less likely to rise up to hit a crankbait or a grub. Again, tubes are the bait of choice and the name of the game is to fish very slowly. If you think you are retrieving the tube slowly enough, back off your retrieve even more.

Lethargic smallmouth will hit a tube one time and then refuse the bait another. Regardless of how slowly you retrieve the tube, smallmouth just won't commit to the tube. Some anglers opt to use a smaller tube but I prefer to modify my tube. I will cut off half of the tube's skirt. This will put the back of the hook closer to the edge of the tube. This will increase the odds of the smallmouth sucking in the tube far enough so you can set the hook. When setting the hook make sure your line is taught. Slack line on a hookset will result in a missed smallmouth.

There is no consistent pattern to catch post-spawn smallmouth. When post-spawn smallmouth hold tight in deep water they are far from easy to catch, but they are not impossible. It is important to use your locator to find smallmouth and you will need to position your boat so your presentation falls as close to the fish as possible, often right in their mouth.

Post-spawn

Remember, the deeper a post-spawn smallmouth is the less aggressive they are. Put in your time and you will be successful.

Chapter 7
Summer River Smallmouth

Fishing on a natural lake or reservoir in summer can be lots of fun, but also frustrating. Just when you think you have figured out a pattern the bite hits a bulkhead. A wind shift, overzealous pleasure boaters, a mile high sky or a cold front can shut down the fishing for an undetermined period of time. Even worse, smallmouth can suddenly develop lockjaw even under ideal conditions.

Being a full time professional fishing guide I have to put the odds in favor of my clients and that is why most of the summer I can be found fishing for river smallmouth. While there is never a sure thing, fishing for summer river smallmouth is as good as it gets. Summer smallmouth bass action on a river can be both exhilarating and predictable, and a pleasure for any fishing guide.

Along with finding active smallmouth for my clients I need to make the catching as basic and effective as possible. My expertise and experience makes me recommend the *wacky worm* for producing consistent catches of summer river smallmouth. The wacky worm has revolutionized the way I fish. In the old days, prior to the wacky worm, I would fish a variety of different techniques and usually find the best presentation for the day through trial and error. This often would take considerable time and affect the days' productivity. While guiding these days, I usually start out at least one of my clients with a wacky worm while the other will throw a topwater bait or soft plastic minnow style jerkbait. On a typical day, it does not take very long for everyone in the boat to be throwing a wacky worm unless there is a good top-water bite.

One advantage to using a wacky worm is that it will catch river smallmouth in a variety of structures while other presentations might only work around one type of structure. I like to start out in the mornings fishing grass edges and will have my client cast tight to the grass. If the smallmouth are holding in the grass then I will switch to the same stick bait but I will rig it Texas style. After we catch all the smallmouth in the grass we usually cast wacky worms tight to shoreline cover. If smallmouth are holding tight to cover I will have my clients tie on a weedless wacky worm hook. Many times by letting the wacky worm sink it will drop into the deeper wood which will hold the big smallmouth.

Even though a stick bait sinks, many times you will need to add some weight to get the bait down to deep cover. On windy days and in current, a non-weighted stick bait does not sink very well. A few manufacturers make weighted hooks and jigheads for wacky worm fishing but I rely on weighting the stick bait. Since I already rig my wacky worm with an O-ring, I like to add a bit of lead to my worm to help it sink. What I do is buy a roll of plumbers solder and cut ½ inch to one inch strips and insert them into the center of the worm. This added weight will cause the worm to fall faster but won't impair the action.

Most of the rivers I fish contain stained water. Watermelon red, green pumpkin/gold flake and green pumpkin/copper flake stick baits are my most productive colors. On some days smallmouth will prefer minnow imitation stick baits and that is why I also bring along some white and pearl hologram.

I also fish a lot of mid-river structure in summer that is perfect for the wacky worm. This mid- river structure contains a mix of rock, logs, grass, and most of all, foraging smallmouth. Smallmouth can be sitting at different levels in the water column. Topwater baits can be hot at times but there are many days when the fish just will not rise to hit a bait on the surface. My records show that about 80 percent of the time I can catch smallmouth with a wacky worm so it is definitely my go-to bait. The reason the wacky worm is so effective is its ability to drop to all levels in the water column. So at whatever depth the smallmouth are holding, if they won't rise to strike a bait the wacky worm will find them.

Big summer smallmouth that hit a wacky worm

I will position the boat so I can drift slowly downstream with the head of my 24 volt MinnKota trolling motor pointed to the rear of the boat. This enables me to control the speed of the drift or hold the boat in place if need be. I have my clients cast at a 45 degree angle down-stream. As the stick bait sinks, I tell them to hold the rod in the 10 o'clock position and to reel in the slack and watch the line. Most of the time a smallmouth will hammer the bait and set the hook on its own. If no strike is detected and the stick bait drops to the bottom, I tell them to raise the rod and again let the stick bait sink. By the time the bait ends up behind the boat it is time for a new cast. This is a simple method and even novice anglers will catch fish. When river smallmouth are aggressive there is no presentation that can come close to this for sheer numbers. My personal favorite was a day when I and two clients boated 122 smallmouth with this method in one day.

River smallmouth will hit a variety of presentations, but given the choice I prefer to fish them on top. I have yet to meet an angler who does not like to catch smallmouth bass on topwater baits. With the exception of muskies, a big smallmouth hitting a topwater bait may be the ultimate thrill in freshwater. After you catch a few smallmouth on top it is hard to switch to another bait. Some anglers would rather catch one or two smallmouth on top than several fish with other presentations.

The best topwater action will occur under stable weather conditions. Simply put, if you have a hot summer with few weather changes the topwater bite can be awesome. However, when we experience a cool summer with continuous cold fronts, the topwater bite can be unpredictable and even non-existent. On an average summer in the Northwoods we see a good topwater bite from late May through mid-September but it peaks during mid to late summer.

Fishing For Smallmouth Bass

While it might seem easy at times, the trick is in knowing when to fish a specific type of structure. On some days it will seem like you can't do anything wrong and you will be on active smallmouth from the time you launch your boat until you return back to the boat landing. However, the reality is that if you count on luck, you might as well play the lottery. Basically what you need to do is fish topwater lures in high percentage areas at the right time. If you fish smart you can make a habit out of catching big river smallmouth on top during the summer.

One an average summer morning, I will start my clients fishing shaded shoreline, downed wood and weeds on the edge of the current. While all these areas can hold smallmouth, on any given day one area will be most productive. There is no secret formula to unlock the mystery of what spot will be most productive.

That said, when push comes to shove, my first stop is the weeds. Why? Because when smallmouth are roaming weeds they are on the feed! Feeding smallmouth are active smallmouth and they will find it hard to pass up a topwater lure on a warm summer morning. If there is a weed bite it won't take long to figure it out.

It is important to approach the weeds with caution especially if you are looking for big smallmouth. Many river fishermen make the mistake of fishing too fast. If your trolling motor is on high or you are drifting too fast you will not only spook larger smallmouth but you will not be able to concentrate on the food chain. Keep your eyes open for not only rising smallmouth but surfacing bait fish. A few surfacing baitfish can advertise that several big smallmouth are in the area.

Zero in on the commotion and cast your topwater bait at the target since your odds to connect with big smallmouth are high. There is no need score a bull's-eye but you need to be ready for the strike. Once the lure hits the water, try to keep a tight line. It is irrelevant as to the bait you are using since you can expect the strike to occur shortly after the bait hits the water. Often the strike will occur before you get a chance to start your retrieve. If you don't get a response with a topwater bait, try a soft plastic jerkbait or a stick bait rigged wacky style.

After the weeds my next stop would be a shaded shoreline with cover. Many river smallmouth will move to deeper water or shoreline cover after dark. As the sun rises they will remain in that cover, and while not catchable at night, they will respond to a surface bait before the sun is high. A 20-inch smallmouth can be in shallow water and aggressively strike a surface lure. The smallmouth that moved to cover at night that is exposed to the sun in the morning will migrate away from the cover. If the cover breaks to deeper water, smallmouth will move deeper and tighter to the cover and won't respond to a surface bait.

By mid-morning, those same shaded shorelines, and weeds will continue to produce smallmouth, but the odds of catching a smallmouth over 18 inches are greatly decreased. Not that catching a bunch of smallmouth between 12-16 inches is a bad thing, but if you are hunting for a big fish it might be time to take a boat ride.

To put the odds in your favor, I suggest heading upstream to shallower water and more current. In summer it is common during the heat of the day to find big smallmouth relating to submerged grass in the center of the river as long as there is sufficient current. The grass supplies plenty of shade along with a forage base of both minnows and crayfish, with the current supplying much needed oxygen once the water rises over 72 degrees.

Once you start fishing the grass it should not take long to find active smallmouth. One unforgettable late summer day the fishing was tough and I knew it was time to head for my honey hole. I started up the motor and we took a short ride upstream to one of my favorite hot spots. The spot had everything a big smallmouth could ask for; rocks, grass, plenty of shade and a downed pine tree. Knowing that this was a prime spot my clients began casting topwater lures before I could put down the trolling motor to help slow down the drift.

Once the boat was positioned properly with my electric trolling motor, I watched as my client made a cast tight to the edge of a downed oak tree. The water exploded and I saw this massive smallmouth roll and wrap itself around a submerged branch. Big smallmouth have this tendency, that when hooked, they move tight to cover. The problem was not that the fish moved to cover but that he had wrapped the line around a branch.

Thanks to my 24 volt trolling motor I was able to move towards the tree as my client kept a tight line. We got lucky, the big smallmouth rolled over the submerged branch and untangled the line. Although the fight continued eventually the fish was in the net. We did not weigh the 21-inch smallmouth but it was easily over 5 1/2 pounds. This is a trophy at any time but especially on a topwater lure. Yes, this is one of those days I will cherish for years.

Over the years the late summer period has proven to be one of the most consistent topwater bites. Even in years when topwater smallmouth are few and far between the action picks up in late summer. If the action is good all summer then it tends to be incredible by late August and early

Fishing For Smallmouth Bass

September. With the exception of an early fall cold front which will bring hostile northwest winds the topwater bite is almost a sure thing.

The cool nights will cause the water temperature to drop sharply in the shallow stained river water. In spring, a drop in the water temperature will drive smallmouth deep or push them tight to submerged cover and spread lockjaw throughout the river. A drop in the water temperature overnight will push river smallmouth tight to shallow wood cover or weeds but they are on the feed.

On a cool late summer morning in the northwoods my first stop would be a patch of grass or milfoil just out of the current. Big smallmouth will move into the vegetation at dusk after feeding, with the largest fish holding right on the seam of the current. While they will strike at a bait, they are a bit lethargic and are seldom in a chasing mood. So a properly placed popper, prop bait or frog teased along the edge of the seam can trigger a strike from a behemoth smallmouth.

Try to position your boat so that your cast will allow the surface lure to move along the seam. Once you move the lure outside the seam you are out of the strike zone. As the lure moves out of the strike zone reel in and make another cast. Trust me, the big ones don't like to chase early in the day. Once the water temperature rises as the morning progresses, the game changes and they will be more aggressive, at that time continue to retrieve back to the boat.

The Hubs Chub is an excellent topwater bait in mid-summer. One year the topwater bite was at its peak the first few weeks of August and we had the smallmouth patterned to the 'T'. The topwater bite would start out slow and we would catch most of the smallmouth early in the day with wacky worms. By mid-day the topwater bite would explode. My old reliable Hubs Chub was the hot bait but we had to fish it slowly. Patience was the key and after casting the Hubs Chub, my clients had to let the bait drop vertically into the water and then give it a short pop. After the pop, you had to let the Hubs Chub fall vertically and after 10-15 seconds make another pop. Just like in the spring, the fact that there is always a bit of movement with the hubs chub when it drops vertically in the water makes it irresistible to any respectable smallmouth. One particularly great day we boated around 75 chunky smallmouth on this presentation. The best topwater action was from 12 noon through 3 pm.

Much of the success rate of a guide's client depends on the client's eagerness to listen to the guide. Most people are on the water to have a good time and are eager to learn. However, after 30 years of guiding I still get the occasional client who prefers to use his favorite baits and does not respond to my suggestions. I have never figured out why people like this hire a guide. Of course, at the end of the day, their poor catch rate is the guide's fault and had nothing to do with them being pigheaded.

A case in point was one August when I had that fantastic topwater bite going on the Menominee River. After a few days of stable weather a small summer cold front passed and I knew that the topwater bite would slow down. Making matters worse, my clients for the next few days were contrarians and had their own way to catch smallmouth. We started out fishing with wacky rigged four-inch Case Magic Sticks and tubes. The bite was slow early in the day but improved as the morning progressed. I could see my clients were getting anxious to fish topwater, since they both said they did not like to fish plastics.

I told them that one of them should tie on a topwater bait. Now, these guys had fished with me before, and I knew that the one guy in particular had no patience for pause and stop retrieve. His idea of fishing topwater was to bulge his buzz bait as fast as possible making about six casts to my one. While they insisted that I did not fish, I made a few casts with a Hubs Chub to show them the proper retrieve. On the second cast I connected with a nice 18 inch smallmouth and I retired my rod.

Most of my clients would have asked for one of the baits I had just caught the smallmouth on, but not this guy. A buzzbait went flying over my head, landed in a downed tree and the buzz bait was doing its thing, not catching any smallmouth. Finally, I convinced him to tie on a Hubs Chub and he caught a few smallmouth. However, he said he did not like to fish this way, went back to the buzzbait and caught no fish. Here is a case where if my clients would have left their tackle boxes at home and used my baits of choice we would have put more fish in the boat.

Although most of my smallmouth fishing is with the three inch Hubs Chub the four inch bait can be a real sleeper for monster summer smallmouth. While it is a great bait for river smallmouth the four inch bait excels on natural lakes when there is a chop on the water. Smallmouth will move atop points and humps under windy conditions. The windier the conditions, the harder you should work the bait over the structure. This method really seems to drive the big smallmouth crazy and will produce incredible strikes.

Buzzbaits are a fantastic choice when river smallmouth are foraging in the weeds during low light conditions. By low light conditions I am referring to dawn, dusk and overcast days. Fishing after dark is a totally different animal. When dealing with these hyper aggressive smallmouth the accuracy of your cast is a critical component to your success. It is critical to keep the buzzbait in the strike zone as long as possible. Most anglers make the mistake of zeroing in on the surfacing bait fish and even if they make what they think is a perfect cast, they can be bypassing the mother lode. You do have a good chance for an immediate strike or having a smallmouth follow the retrieve. If your cast falls short, the odds are slim that you will be able to pull a big smallmouth away from the restaurant. Long casts can result in wasted time since, unlike largemouth, smallmouth don't tend to bury themselves in the weeds.

The ideal presentation would be to over cast the weedline about ten feet and start your retrieve as the bait hits the water keeping your bait in the strike zone for the maximum amount of time. This retrieve will also catch a higher percentage of larger smallmouth. One hot humid July I turned a client on to this technique and we were able to boat several big smallmouth. My client was one of those guys that was addicted to buzz baits since his expertise was wading small streams and rivers. The topwater bite was on and I wanted my client to catch the maximum number of fish; the buzz bait would be the bait of choice.

Typical of an angler used to fishing small clear streams, my client was adamant about making long casts with a 1/8 ounce buzzbait. Even though we were fishing a weedline his casts were falling well back into the weeds, and even though he did catch a smallmouth none of them were over 15 inches. While I suggested that he direct his cast just past the inner edge of the weeds, and look for irregularities in the weeds, my words fell on deaf ears. Being a considerate guide I knew I had to teach my client a new technique but not be too pushy.

I took off my Hubs Chub and tied on a white 3/8 ounce buzzbait and got to work. I prefer to use a slightly heavier rod when fishing a buzzbait than when fishing with a prop bait like a Hubs Chub, but I was quick to get that buzz bait in the water. With my client in the front of the boat and getting first shot at any potential predator, I positioned the boat parallel to the weedline and stressed one more time that my client only needed to cast just into the inside edge of the weeds. After he made two casts without a strike I made one cast over the inner edge of a small weed spike that protruded out a few feet from the weedline. A 19 inch smallmouth hammered the buzzbait after one turn of the reel. Obviously my client heard the surface explosion and saw the big airborne smallmouth, but he didn't realize where I had caught the fish. He yelled, "What color buzzbait were you using?"

After I boated and released the smallmouth I showed him the weed point where I caught the big smallmouth and told him that my choice of color was irrelevant. I did suggest that he put on a larger buzzbait. After he tied on a 1/4 ounce white buzzbait I watched his next cast fall a few feet into the weeds and to my satisfaction a big smallmouth exploded on the surface. The big smallmouth would be the first of many that afternoon on the Menominee River. I guess some people just need to see results before they modify their techniques. Anyway, the adjustments made for a great day on the water and a very happy client.

What size buzzbait is best for smallmouth? On most occasions smallmouth prefer a smaller buzzbait than largemouth bass but much will depend on the type of water you are fishing, the conditions and the average size of the smallmouth that inhabits the water you are fishing. A 1/4 ounce will work fine under most situations whether you are fishing on a lake, reservoir or river. For a small river or stream smallmouth a 1/8 ounce buzzbait might be your best option since big smallmouth are rare in these waters. Small streams are also usually clear in summer and the smallmouth are skittish. A long cast with a 1/8 ounce buzzbait will get the most strikes. If I'm fishing big fish water a 1/4 buzzbait is my favorite for smallmouth. If there is a good chop on the water or I am specifically looking for a big smallmouth a 3/8 ounce buzzbait is your best bet.

What about trailer hooks? For the most part I do not use trailer hooks on buzzbaits mainly due to the increase of snags, particularly with weeds and grass. On the other hand I know many smallmouth anglers that never throw a buzzbait that does not have a trailer hook. If you are fishing and missing more smallmouth than you are catching then you might want to tie on a trailer hook.

Unlike poppers and prop baits smallmouth are not as apt to chase a buzzbait with bright skies, air temperatures pushing 90 degrees and not so much as a ripple on the river. To catch river smallmouth under these conditions you will need to concentrate on cover and shade. Each cast will need to be carefully placed so that the bulk of your retrieve will chug along in the shade. You will need to position your boat so you can make your cast parallel to the shoreline. However, I again stress that a popper or a prop bait will catch more fish. The buzzbait does have the advantage of being able to be fished tighter to cover.

I use both spinning and bait casting tackle when fishing buzzbaits depending on the size of the buzzbait and type of cover. If I am fishing a

Fishing For Smallmouth Bass

free flowing stretch of river with rocks, grass, and shoreline wood a spinning rod can work just fine for most anglers. My ideal spinning rod is a six foot six or seven foot medium to medium heavy rod. Spool your medium retrieve spinning reel with 20 pound braided line. The braided line will allow for longer casts and immediate hook penetration.

When using a spinning rod I like to keep my rod tip pointed at the buzzbait. This will result in less slack in the line putting me in direct contact to the bait. If there is too much slack or if your rod tip is too soft the result will be short strikes, leaving the angler to think that the bass are just hitting the buzzbait's skirt. These so called short strikes are usually a combination of operator error and mismatched equipment. You will never be able to completely eliminate short strikes but if you tweak your tackle you will hook more smallmouth.

There are a few tricks to casting a buzzbait that, along with casting accuracy, can make you catch more fish. One trick that is essential to learn is to close the bail just before the buzzbait hits the water, which is easy when using a spinning reed. This subtle habit makes sure that the buzzbait has started its retrieve immediately. If you fail to apply immediate pressure you will miss more fish than you catch on most days. This is a common occurrence for novice anglers.

How and when you set the hook is an important aspect to successful buzzbait fishing. When reeling in the buzzbait it is important to focus totally on the bait. When a strike occurs, I lower my rod and watch which way the line moves. Then, when the line tightens, set the hook home in the opposite direction. If the line is not tight before you set the hook you will miss more fish than you hook.

I like to switch to a Chug bug when the topwater bite fades or smallmouth are hitting short. If you are fishing with a partner and the topwater bite slows down, one angler should tie on a Chug Bug.

A Chug Bug can be made to "walk the dog" but there is less room for error than other topwater lures like the Zara Spook or the four inch Hubs Chub. After the cast, face the lure and hold your rod almost straight down and close to the water. Reel most, but not all, of the slack out of your line and give your rod a jerk. Here is where most people encounter a problem. Too little slack and you will simply rip the bait straight through the water. Too much slack and the bait won't move when you jerk. What should happen when you jerk the rod is the head of the Chug Bug should move side to one side. Here is where timing becomes important. While the head of the Chug Bug is still to one side and before the tension on the line pulls the lure back straight, jerk the rod again. Done properly, this will swing the head of the Chug Bug to the other side. The Chug Bug tends to develop more slack in the line than other topwater lures and the angler needs to concentrate on their timing as they jerk the rod. This is accomplished by turning the reel handle to maintain the proper tension.

Like most topwater lures, the Chug Bug is a fun bait to fish and a few should be in every serious anglers' tackle box. It comes in three different sizes. The Baby Bug is small but is deadly on small streams. The original Chug Bug is 3/8 oz. and is great for all types of water. If you are on big fish waters don't hesitate to cast the Big Chug Bug.

Another popular topwater bait for river smallmouth anglers is the Heddon Tiny Torpedo.   I have had my best success buzzing it across the surface in the heat of summer. Try to keep your cast as low to the surface of the water as possible and close the bail as the bait hits the surface. Once it hits the surface, give the Torpedo a quick twitch and start buzzing it across the surface. Don't pause the bait even if you get a strike. Again, due to the Torpedo's smaller size, if a smallmouth strikes short it will usually strike the bait a second time. It is important to retrieve the bait all the way back to the boat.

The Tiny Torpedo is also a good choice for fishing weeds early and late in the day. During low light conditions both popping and buzzing presentations work. Usually I will start out by buzzing the Tiny Torpedo over the weeds looking for active smallmouth. If I am missing strikes or don't get any response I will revert to popping the Tiny Torpedo.

If I am fishing in current the "do nothing" retrieve can be very productive. What I do is cast the Tiny Torpedo upstream, keep a tight line and watch. When it hits the water I give it a fast pop and let it drift downstream. I will occasionally give it a pop and again keep a tight line and watch the lure. River smallmouth will follow the lure and the soft pop will trigger the strike. The "do nothing" retrieve will take plenty of patience and you need to concentrate on the lure but it can be deadly under bright skies at mid-day.

The Tiny Torpedo is popular for smallmouth anglers who wade small streams. While I do very little wading for smallmouth there is one place on the Menominee River where wading is the only way to put me up close and personal with big smallmouth. There is a set of rapids and a waterfall that are inaccessible to any watercraft. When water levels drop in summer the cooler highly oxygenated water attracts schools of baitfish and plenty of smallmouth.

Dragging a tube across humps, rocks, or the river bottom can be a very deadly presentation, since it imitates the movement of a crayfish. When an angler drags a tube, he should also know the habits of the crayfish. For the most part, crayfish will crawl horizontally along the bottom. If you have ever watched crayfish move along the bottom they will exhibit sudden bursts of speed but for the most part they are lethargic as they move along the bottom. A bass will monitor the crayfish movements and go in for the kill when it pauses.

When I drag a tube, I am in the mindset that there is a live crayfish on the end of my line. The only thing that I do differently than most anglers is I don't let the tube sit motionless on the bottom. After I pause the tube, I slowly reel in the slack, and when the line is taught, I raise the rod tip a few inches and slowly drop it back down. What this does is cause the tentacles of the tube to quiver which resembles the legs of the crayfish. A smallmouth cruising the rocks will find the tube irresistible. Even though most tubes on the market are heavily salted and scented, it never hurts to add a little added scent to your tube. The scent won't attract the smallmouth but it can cause the bass to hang on to the tube longer and increase your rate of hook sets.

While it is not difficult to learn, many anglers don't have enough patience to fish a tube properly under all conditions. If the smallmouth are aggressive, there is no need to quiver the tube on the lake or river bottom. But if the bite is light the ability to coax a wary smallmouth will work to your advantage.

Tubes can be rigged a variety of different ways and it still amazes me how many times I have seen smallmouth caught with tubes rigged in the most bizarre way, especially when fishing on a river. One summer day I had a client fishing with me who along with having limited fishing knowledge had never fished with a tube before. I assured him that fishing a tube was not rocket science and that by mid-day he would be catching bass like a pro. What I did not expect was my client to show the guide a new way to fish a tube.

We started fishing a rocky shoreline looking for smallmouth to be foraging on crayfish. It took a while but eventually my client caught his first smallmouth bass on a tube. I grabbed the fish and after I released it into the water I inspected the tube and told my client that it was critical that he check the tube after catching a fish to ensure it was rigged properly.

My client caught a few more fish and I also got into the action. However, the action came to an abrupt halt. We must have fished for at least 45 minutes without a strike. I switched to a grub and after observing my clients' ragged tube I told him that it was time for a fresh tube.

I reached into my bag of tricks and pulled out a fresh tube and told my client to pass me his rod. My client said, "No need for that, I can rig up my own tube". I thought, "No problem," tossed him the tube and made a cast with my grub. I had no response with my grub and was ready to change baits when my client yelled, "Got one!"

Not only did he have a smallmouth, but it was by far the largest fish of the morning. As I slid the net under the 19 incher I noticed that something about the tube looked funny. As I grabbed the fish I noticed that the tube was reversed on the jighead. My client had placed the hook of the jighead through the nose of the tube with the eye of the jig protruding through the tentacles.

I was dumbfounded! How do you tell a client who just caught the largest fish of the morning that he rigged the tube the wrong way? I suppose that some guides would have demeaned the client and told them they just got lucky, but being an inquisitive angler, I thought to myself, let's try this again. Was it just a freak or was this greenhorn on to something. So for the moment I said nothing, hoping my client would repeat the procedure and catch another bass.

It was hard for me to watch my client without making him feel on edge with me staring at him. I was trying to monitor his expert presentation so if need be I could duplicate it. If my client had caught a 15 inch smallmouth it would not have been a big deal, but when someone catches a 19 incher, you try to figure out if it was a fluke or a definite pattern. Just as I was convincing myself that it was a fluke, my client ripped into another big smallmouth.

After I released my clients' second big smallmouth, I figured it was time to tell him that his method of rigging tubes was contrary to mine. I asked him if there was a reason for his method and he said, "No, I just figured that it didn't matter how it was hooked."

In summer I have also had good success wacky rigging a tube and letting it drift weightless over mid-river rocks and grass. The tube will float or sink only inches below the surface and on some days smallmouth will eat them like popcorn. Since I am not using an expensive jighead and snags are minimal even in mega rocky areas, it is an easy technique for even an inexperienced angler but one that seasoned bassers should also add to their arsenal.

What I do is cast the tube upstream over rocks and grass, let the tube drift downstream and, while keeping a tight line, twitch the tube and let it fall. To give the tube a bit of weight I will add a tiny BB sized split shot just above the eye of the hook. As far as a hook goes you can use either an octopus hook or a Kahle hook. This method has worked on days when smallmouth for whatever reason were hitting the soft plastic stick baits lightly and my clients were having trouble setting the hook. It also works very well with overzealous kids.

I have caught plenty of big river smallmouth in summer using soft plastic jerkbaits. While they are effective in all types of cover they shine when fished around wood cover and weeds. While soft plastic jerkbaits remain effective when smallmouth are relating to wood cover it is an essential part of my arsenal when fishing mid river weeds. I use both floating and sinking jerkbaits when fishing river grass depending on both the current and density of the grass. If the grass is thick, I will use an unweighted jerkbait rigged on a wide gap hook and let the bait drift over the grass. Big smallmouth will hide under the grass on bright sunny days, similar to the way a big largemouth will find comfort under slop. Smallmouth will strike a surface bait, but the treble hooks will pick up grass before you even start your retrieve.

My technique is simple, as you drift downstream make a cast on a 45 degree angle downstream. With a high speed retrieve reel, reel in the slack and lower your rod tip and give the bait vigorous twitches. These erratic movements will look like surfacing baitfish feeding on insects or smaller baitfish. Keep the line as taught as possible and make sure you feel the fish on the line before setting the hook. This method has resulted in many 20-inch river smallmouth in summer. Although I prefer to move the jerkbait drifting over the weeds, I have had many of my clients catch smallmouth doing nothing but just allowing the jerkbait to drift. This will work as long as you keep a taught line to set the hook.

When I am guiding I will have one or both of my clients fishing over the grass with the unweighted jerkbait and I will work a weighted jerkbait like a Case Sinking Minnow or a wacky worm along the edge of the grass. This way we are able to cover the grass effectively and adapt accordingly. On a typical summer day on the river we usually use both presentations hand in hand.

Soft plastic frogs are ideal for fishing river grass, sparse weed patches, log jams, or any heavy cover. These frogs will usually disrupt more water than the hollow bodied and are best fished with a constant retrieve. You can vary the speed during your retrieve but if you stop the frog will sink. Soft bodied frogs are usually rigged "texposed," meaning the hook is Texas rigged with the tip of the point tucked just under the surface of the lure. A texposed solid body frog is weedless and snag proof.

I have had my best success fishing soft bodied frogs over river grass. I started using frogs one hot summer due to the excess surface grass. There was a good topwater bite but both our poppers and prop baits were consistently picking up grass. If you did not get a strike the first few feet of your retrieve you had to quickly retrieve the bait, shake off the grass and recast. Making matters worse, the smallmouth were holding tight in the grass and if the surface bait fell short of the grass it was a wasted cast.

The smallmouth were hitting on top but I didn't want to switch to a soft plastic jerkbait which would not get hung up in the grass. Sure, the jerkbait would have caught fish, but the adrenaline level would be much lower.

I don't know if it was out of frustration or what but I grabbed a soft plastic frog out of my bag of tricks and rigged it on a wide gap hook. It must have taken about a half a dozen casts but I eventually hooked a nice smallmouth. I remember telling my client before I caught the smallmouth that even if I wasn't catching anything at least I wasn't getting hung up on the grass. The truth is I probably would have kept using the frog for at least a half hour before I threw in the towel. The rest of the day we caught smallmouth on poppers, prop baits and the frog. The frog had the advantage since it was in the strike zone longer being that it was grass free.

Ever since that day I have been using the frog on the river and it is hard to beat when smallmouth are holding in the grass. Just as when fishing a buzzbait, it is important to start your retrieve as soon as the frog hits the water. As the frog hits the water give it a fast pop and quickly reel in the slack and hold on. If you don't get a strike buzz the frog for about two feet and give it another pop. Next, I slow it down, being careful to keep the frog on the surface and again start buzzing the frog about one foot. I have coaxed many big smallmouth out of the grass by popping a frog even at high noon with blue skies in the heat of summer. Big smallmouth love to hide under river grass to avoid the sun and on many occasions the bait to trigger a strike is a frog.

Popping the frog does not always trigger a strike and you might need to keep the frog moving but vary the retrieve. Smallmouth will occasionally hit the frog as your retrieve slows down but most of the strikes will occur when you speed up the retrieve. If that does not trigger a strike try letting the frog fall when you encounter an opening in the grass. Let the frog drop for about ten seconds and if no strike is felt continue buzzing the frog. I like to give the frog a pop before I continue my retrieve.

Prior to the revolution in soft plastic that has occurred over the past 20 years, floating crankbaits were the staple of river anglers. In fact, to this day I see many anglers fishing on rivers who use only floating crankbaits. It might be that these people don't take too kindly to change, or they could be catching fish and find no need to change. It is probably a combination of the two, but the bottom line is that a properly placed floating crankbait will catch lots of river smallmouth just like they did 30 years ago.

Ask a dozen river anglers how to fish a floating crankbait and you will get a dozen different answers. One method, which is my favorite, is to slowly fish the first few feet tight to the shoreline or cover then retrieve the lure with a series of "snaps" and "tugs" back to the boat. This method works great when the smallmouth are active; there's something about this fast twitch method that drives smallmouth wild! When smallmouth are aggressive you really can't work this bait too fast for the speedy smallmouth, and I've found that the more erratic you work the bait, the better the results will be. Experiment with long tugs, short tugs and varying lengths of pauses until you find out what mood the smallmouth are in. On some days I will pause in the middle of the retrieve and let the rings settle before continuing.

A Big Smallmouth that hammered a shallow running crankbait

Some anglers like to only focus on the shoreline and surrounding cover. They will make a cast, let the rings settle and give the bait a "snap." Next, they will let the bait settle again and repeat the procedure a few more times before making another shoreline cast. This works great when fishing shaded shorelines or steep banks with wood cover. However, if the bank does not break to deeper water the angler could be missing smallmouth by not fishing the bait back to the boat.

I know many anglers that will tie a suspending jerkbait on one rod and a floating crankbait on another. At first glance they look similar and for a novice angler it is difficult to tell them apart. When the average angler casts the suspending jerkbait they will retrieve the lure back to the boat and often catch a smallmouth at boatside. It baffles me why they will cast the floating crankbait with the same color pattern as the suspending jerkbait and only work the shoreline. I guess they like missing fish!

It is common knowledge that in summer you can catch smallmouth by twitching a floating crankbait tight to shoreline cover. However, many anglers fail to utilize this presentation when fishing mid-river rocks.

Fishing For Smallmouth Bass

Mid-river rocks always have the potential to hold big smallmouth and a rising crankbait that breaks the surface can result in a 20 inch river smallmouth in the hands of a patient angler. While it might not be my first choice I never leave a prime area without trying a few casts. It can salvage a slow day of fishing or a day when the bite on other topwater baits shuts down.

One day I was fishing with two clients and we were having an exceptional morning on the Menominee River. The guy in the front of the boat was catching smallmouth with a bone/shad pattern three inch Hubs Chub. His partner in the rear of the boat was using a Pop-R and was also having fantastic success. We were fishing shorelines, grass and rocks and it did not matter since the topwater bite was on big time. It was looking like it was going to be one of those days you dream about.

Suddenly we hit a bulkhead and the bite shut down. We even switched to wacky worms and soft plastic jerkbaits but had no response. It was like every smallmouth in the river had suddenly vanished. After fumbling around in my bag of tricks I pulled out a fire tiger floating Rapala. I made a few casts towards the rock and grass in the middle of the river and eventually was tangling with a dandy 16 inch smallmouth. My clients both looked and almost on cue, both asked if I had any more of them. I gladly honored their request and they got into the action. That is why I always carry a few floating crankbaits in the boat.

The only problem that can arise is that summer river smallmouth can be just about anywhere. You can pattern them on one day and return to the same spot the next day, only to find no fish. When you find smallmouth the odds are in your favor to catch them, but you will need to hunt for them. For covering water and searching for mobile smallmouth it is hard to beat a crankbait. Few other baits will allow you to cover water and different depths.

Although you need to cover water, it is important to slow down when you approach classic rock structure. Both the upstream and downstream edge of the rocks can hold lots of smallmouth, so it warrants some quality time. Spend time and work the area effectively because there are times when this area can hold the mother lode, salvaging many a slow day.

One hot July day I was fishing with 2 clients from Pennsylvania. They had caught some big smallmouth before but never any number of them on any given day. We had fished many of my favorite spots and could not connect with a smallmouth over 17 inches. Not only were big fish avoiding us but we could not catch more than three smallmouth in any one spot. It looked like just one of those days; we were catching fish, but nothing to write home about.

We were drifting over 9 feet of water with a sand and muck bottom and I told my clients to tie on crankbaits that would run down to six feet. I knew as we approached the rock ledge we would find some fish, so I told them to get ready. I positioned the bow of the boat into the current and watched my locater for the ledge. Once the boat was over the ledge, I held the boat directly over the ledge with my trolling motor.

After a few casts we boated a 19 inch smallmouth, and before we got it to the boat the other guy had another big fish on. They were both casting on opposite sides of the boat, telling us that these fish were scattered all along the ledge. We continued to catch a fish ever few minutes and when the action slowed I just moved the boat back and forth along the ledge. All the fish were caught tight to the ledge. If the cast was away from the ledge even 10 feet, well, there were no fish.

We ended up with over 20 smallmouth between 18 and 20 inches; incredible in anyone's standards. Those big smallmouth were holding on the rock ledge right on the current break. If we would have just drifted over the ledge we may not have caught any fish at all. We continued to fish other areas and reverted back to the occasional medium sized smallmouth.

These edges have produced many big smallmouth in summer. The key is to find a rock ledge with a good current. A rock ledge or hump in slack water or slow current will not attract big smallmouth in summer. The lower the water levels get the more fish that can stack up along these ledges. Low water levels make fishing a ledge easier but you will need to use caution. One thing is for certain, there is no better way to catch these rock smallmouth than with a crankbait.

Besides ledges, also look for changes in the rocks. Any changes, with a variety of different sized rock, can hold tons of crayfish. On several occasions I have caught a few scattered smallmouth on a rock shelf, come to an abrupt change in the rock, and started catching lots of fish. Besides attracting crayfish these areas also act as a transition. Anytime you find a transition area, near an area that is already holding fish, you can expect to find a good concentration of fish. Mix in a few weeds and it will be a magnet for a big fish.

If you are targeting big smallmouth then you need to target big fish areas. Look for rock that is adjacent to a slough and deep water to attract the largest river smallmouth. If you find an area with an incoming creek, deep water and rocks the spot should have big fish written all over it. Any big boulder on the edge of the creek channel is a magnet for a big fish. Also look for isolated boulders up stream or downstream from the creek channel.

As far as live bait goes, nightcrawlers are also hard to beat in summer. While I have had some success with leeches I usually don't bother to bring them along. Why are nightcrawlers so effective? It is because when a smallmouth hits a nightcrawler, it thinks it is feeding on a crayfish. While this nightcrawler crayfish connection is no secret, few anglers take advantage of it.

Nightcrawlers can be rigged either on a plain hook or with a light jighead. Both these presentations will work depending on the structure you are fishing and the current. On average, I will have my best success with a plain #4 or #2 Octopus hook with a split shot clinched 12 to 16 inches up from the hook. When fishing a deeper hole I rely on a jig. Chartreuse and orange are two of my favorite jig colors.

When hooking a nightcrawler on a plain hook or a jig, hook the crawler once through the head. Although this is no secret, it amazes me how many anglers will still ball up the nightcrawler. Hooking the nightcrawler once will keep the nightcrawler fresh and lively. Sure you will get some short strikes, but the bottom line is you will get more strikes. Balling up the crawler will often result in lots of strikes from rough fish.

Don't count out live bait for big smallmouth!

Whether you fish a jig or plain hook rig, keep in mind that the nightcrawler is mimicking a crayfish, so it has to make contact with the bottom. Also be prepared for light bites. When smallmouth feed on crayfish they will often nip at the crayfish before zeroing in on the kill. A smallmouth thinking the crawler is a crayfish will nip the crawler, then suck it in. So don't set the hook the instant you feel the strike. Wait five to ten seconds before setting the hook.

Many people think if you use live bait you will cause damage to the smallmouth. This is not true if you use barbless hooks. I will clinch down the barbs on both my plain hooks and jigs. Believe me, besides not harming the fish you will not lose fish. Yes, on occasion you will lose a jumping fish, but you will also lose a jumping fish on a topwater or crankbait.

You will have that occasional slow day on the river in summer but they will be few and far between if you follow the techniques that I have laid out. Don't make fishing complicated and you will have lots of fun on the river in summer.

Chapter 8
Clear Water Smallmouth

If I am fishing a clear water lake for smallmouth and I am hit with a cold front I will usually start and finish the day with a grub. That is not to say that my clients and I don't try other presentations, it is just that the grub shines no matter how challenging the conditions.

It was late July and my clients wanted to catch smallmouth from a lake. We had two great days on the river but one of my clients inquired about fishing smallmouth in a lake. I told them that the smallmouth action is more consistent on the river and that if we fished a lake we might not have very good success. Although my clients knew that the action would not be as good as it had been the last two days on the river, they wanted to learn how to fish clear water lakes for smallmouth in summer.

I picked them up in the morning and I told them we were going to fish a 1,000 acre lake that had a good smallmouth population along with some huge smallmouth. On the way to the boat landing I told them that even though a minor cold front had passed overnight, we still had overcast skies which would work in our favor. I explained that the smallmouth would be either suspending over open water or structure, holding tight to cover or buried in the deep weeds. One of my clients asked what kind of lures we would be using and I quickly replied, "Grubs!"

After I launched the boat I told my clients that it would be trial and error until we found some smallmouth and developed a pattern. I told my clients that the first place we would be heading was a large point, and that I was looking for the smallmouth to be suspended off the deep edge of the point. I killed my outboard about one hundred yards short of the point and put down my electric trolling motor. I gave one client a 3/8 ounce darter head jig and a three inch black grub and the other client a 3/8 ounce darter head jig with a three inch watermelon red grub.

When we got about fifty yards off the point I stopped the boat and grabbed my rod with a 3/8 ounce darter head jig with a three inch green pumpkin grub. I suggested that my clients watch what I do since it is the perfect retrieve after a cold front. I made a long cast with the aid of my seven foot rod and four pound test monofilament line. This was in the days before fluorocarbon line. After the grub hit the water I let it sink for about ten seconds then jerked the rod tip causing the grub to dart rapidly. I then reeled in the grub with a slow steady retrieve. After I retrieved the grub about four cranks of the reel I repeated the jerking action. After I jerked the rod the third time and started my retrieve, I connected with a nice 17 inch smallmouth.

It did not take long for my clients to catch one and the first hour of fishing yielded six nice smallmouth from the deep edge of the point. After we landed the sixth smallmouth the action stopped and I told my clients that we had either caught all the active smallmouth that were suspending off the point or we had caught the only smallmouth suspending off the point. We continued to fish the entire point with grubs and a variety of crankbaits and plastics and could not stick one fish.

We proceeded to another point but the darting technique did not work. After casting several different baits it was obvious that nothing else would work either. Even though we were not catching any smallmouth my electronics showed several schools suspended at various levels; they definitely had lock-jaw. I told my clients that it was time to make another move and that this time we would see if we could snag a few smallmouth out of the weeds.

Our next spot was a deep weed-line. I easily found the weed-line but my electronics showed no fish. I explained to my clients that even though my electronics gave us the impression that no fish were present we were still going to fish the weed-line and that grubs would remain the bait of choice. The big difference would be in the way that we would be presenting the grubs.

I stressed to my clients that after making a long cast parallel to the weed-line, it would be important to let the grub fall to the bottom. After the grub fell to the bottom and they had slack in their line I told my clients to start a steady slow retrieve back to the boat. I positioned my boat so the two anglers could cast as parallel to the weed-line as possible. I also stressed that we did not want to cast into the weeds but just work the grub along the weed edge. Cold front smallmouth have a habit of holding just inside the weeds at the base of the weed-line, and if the grub is too far from the base of the weeds a big smallmouth will not chase it.

It took a while before one of my clients felt life on the end of the line but it was well worth the wait. The guy in the front of the boat commented that he could not tell if he was dragging the bottom or if he was getting light strikes. I told him that due to the cold front that he should not expect hard strikes and that he would need to concentrate and be patient. I added that we were using light line and medium light action rods so a soft hookset would work best. My client was surprised when the next light bite turned out to be a chunky 19 inch smallmouth. They caught several smallmouth by swimming grubs along the deep weedline and every smallmouth ended up pushing 18 inches or better.

Darter head grub jigheads that have the hook eye perpendicular to the hook shank will pick up weeds and on that particular day, I did not have an option. In recent years there have been many innovations in jighead design with several manufacturers designing jigheads with a narrow nose and the hook eye at the tip of the jig. This style of jighead will allow the grub to glide through weeds.

After lunch we returned to the first point where we had had all the early morning action. We tried darting the grub but had no success. I moved closer to the point and my electronics showed a big school of smallmouth suspending about a foot off the bottom. I told my clients to drop the jigs and let them hit bottom, tighten up the line and jig the jig a short hop. They repeated the procedure several times and eventually started catching smallmouth. I told them that if we were using round jigheads the grub would not be sitting horizontal in the water and the smallmouth would not be hitting the grubs. My clients were amazed at how they had caught smallmouth three different ways with the darter head and grub combination.

Grubs can hold their own with any artificial bait once the temperature starts to drop in the fall. Cold water should be approached differently in fall than in spring. In spring, bass activity will increase as water temperatures rise, while in fall, bass activity surges as the water temperatures drop. Spring smallmouth tend to be scattered as they roam shoreline areas searching for food and warm water. By fall, they're ready to put on the feedbag and school up.

Fall fishing may sound easy, but you still need to determine the bite for the day, especially if you are searching for big smallmouth. If you start with a large grub, you may get light strikes from big bass. Once a big bass hits, if he's not hooked, the odds of catching him are slim. If you are catching fish and they are hitting the grub hard, then try a larger grub, since the larger grub may result in larger fish. As the water temperature starts to rise during daylight hours, bass become more active, so the larger grub can become more productive, especially if you are fishing in big fish water.

Smallmouth bass will suspend on many northern lakes in fall and a grub will allow the angler to vary his presentation until they make contact with a school of smallmouth. It is important that you keep a mental note as to how deep into the water column you are letting the grub drop before you start your retrieve. Knowing precisely how deep the smallmouth are holding is important and it is critical that your grub gets into the strike zone.

I like to make a cast and count to five and start my retrieve. This will get me into the strike zone of smallmouth suspending high in the water column. I continue to let my grub fall with intervals of a five count, counting to five, ten, fifteen until contact, if any, is made. I have let my grub drop for as much as 30 seconds before making contact with smallmouth. When the grub gets to the desired depth, I will jig it a short hop and then start a steady retrieve back to the boat. Most of the time a 3/8 ounce or ½ ounce jighead with a four or five inch grub is the best combination.

Color can also be important and anglers should try to match the forage base as much as possible. If smallmouth are feeding on ciscoes or smelt, use grubs that have blue, silver or white. Green pumpkin, pumpkinseed and motor oil might work in spring and summer, but I have not had good success with them when the smallmouth are feeding on ciscoes or smelt.

Experience has taught me that smallmouth can hold tight in deep grass and that when this occurs even the best electronics won't pick them up. I suggest that if you are on a good smallmouth lake, even if you don't mark smallmouth in the deep sand grass, fish it anyway. If I were to only fish for smallmouth that I marked with my electronics, my prediction is that there would be many days when I would either get skunked or put only a few fish in the boat. This is one lesson that I learned the hard way over the years.

After locating a patch of sand grass I position my boat into the wind and use my electric trolling motor to move me slowly over the sand grass. When there is a heavy chop on the water I forget about the sand grass and look for smallmouth elsewhere. If you drift with the wind, what will happen is the boat will drift too swiftly over the sand grass and it will be impossible to find the proper weight. Even if you do find the proper weight, it won't be in the strike zone very long and you will also have trouble detecting a strike. Even for a very skilled angler this can be challenging.

Once I position my boat over the sand grass I cast my Mojo rig into the wind and let it slowly drop into the grass. Be prepared for a quick strike because a suspended smallmouth can strike the rig on the drop. Once the Mojo Rig is on the bottom, slowly lift the tip of your rod, let it fall again and reel up the slack in your line. The slower you can work this rig the better.

If you are not getting any strikes, crawl the rig slowly across the bottom. I have even caught smallmouth dead sticking a Mojo rig, which resembles live bait fishing.

Rigging up a Mojo Rig is easy. All you need to do is slide on a sinker and tie on a 1/0 wide gap hook and peg the weight to the line. The rubber pegs made by the Mojo Tackle Company work fine but they are expensive so I will use a toothpick to peg the Mojo sinker onto the line. Next, choose your bait of choice and slide the pegged weight up the line to whatever leader size you desire. There are a number of plastics that can be used with the Mojo rig when working deep sand grass for smallmouth bass. I prefer to use cylindrical jerkbaits like Yamamoto Senkos, Case Magic Stiks, four and six inch finesse worms and lizards. When working grass or any other cover for that matter, it is important to Texas rig your plastics. If you are fishing an unobstructed bottom you can use an octopus hook.

If there is a chop on the water I will leave the shoreline and the weeds to other anglers and head for the points and humps searching for suspended smallmouth. I have been fishing one particular lake for over 25 years and I have learned that a slider head with a black or grape four inch worm is the easiest way to catch a bunch of smallmouth. Smallmouth will suspend about forty or fifty yards out from the points and are usually suspending about five to ten feet deep in the water column feeding on baitfish. I have never caught a smallmouth over 16 inches but have caught as many as 30 smallmouth off one point. While I catch my fair share with grubs, tubes and crankbaits, the Slider presentation works best.

It is an easy pattern to tap into. If the wind is out of the south or southwest, which is common in summer, head for the point on the north end of the lake. If the wind is out of the east or north which is rare in the summer, the point on the west end of the lake attracts the most smallmouth. The only problem is that an east or north wind is usually the result of a cold front so the bite can be tough. This is where patience and concentration win the day. The slower you retrieve the slider worm the more smallmouth you will catch.

The rock hump in the center of the lake is also a great spot to look for suspended smallmouth. The only problem that I have when fishing the hump is dealing with walleye fisherman who flock to the hump when there is a chop on the water. In fact, on a few occasions I had to refrain from fishing smallmouth due to the over-abundance of walleye fishermen. But the day I remember most was when there were about a dozen walleye anglers on top of the hump and I was the only boat fishing for smallmouth.

Fishing For Smallmouth Bass

The good news was that while the walleyes weren't biting my client was still catching a boat load of smallmouth.

We were catching smallmouth consistently from the weeds and shoreline wood when, about mid-day, the wind started to kick up. The smallmouth shut down and we could not get a strike. Even the points were like fishing in a dead sea. I knew that the only chance I had to put fish in the boat was to head for the mid-lake hump, knowing that I would have to deal with the walleye fishermen.

The hump is five feet below the surface and I told my client that the smallmouth usually suspend 10-30 yards off the hump and five feet below the surface. We were using 1/4 ounce jigheads and black worms with a chartreuse tail. I told my client to make a cast and count to seven as I held the boat off the edge of the hump with my electric trolling motor. On the second cast my client caught a nice 16 inch smallmouth. After my client caught his second smallmouth I got into the action and we lost count of the number of suspended smallmouth we caught, but it was easily over 20. After my client caught about 10 smallmouth, he said that he had been watching the walleye fishermen and that he hadn't seen one walleye caught.

Eventually the smallmouth action stopped and right on cue, the walleyes started to bite. We had brought some leeches along in case the bite was tough. All we had to do was tie on a leadhead jig, tip them with a leech and move in for the kill. So before leaving the hump we got into the walleye action and my client and I ended up with a bonus walleye dinner. Now that, my friend, is the ideal day on the water.

I have caught more suspended smallmouth with Slider worms than any other presentation in the summer. In fall, whether you are fishing a point or a hump, suspended smallmouth continue to hit a Slider worm but crankbaits are more effective. When fall smallmouth hit a crankbait the school will follow the hooked smallmouth back to the boat. However, when I catch a suspended fall smallmouth on a Slider worm I seldom see a school of smallmouth following the hooked fish. This is an interesting observation. The only explanation I have is that the smallmouth see the crankbait in the mouth of the hooked fish and, just as with a live minnow, they go into a frenzy. I have seen this happen often over my many years on the water.

One deadly tactic for catching clear water smallmouth is using a drop shot rig. Drop shotting is not a technique that is difficult to learn as I have found out teaching it to anglers with limited fishing experience. For the most part the bites are hard and relatively easy to detect. If the bass does not strike the bait hard, it will usually push the line off to one side so the angler has to be alert. This is an advantage to using visible line like Yo-Zuri H20. This 100 percent fluorocarbon has a slight green tint that lowers the reflectivity of the line below the surface of the water. However, above the surface of the water the line has reflectivity, allowing the angler to see even the slightest line movement. H20 is a very soft fluorocarbon line that will cast easy and have less memory than other fluorocarbon lines.

Choosing the right rod and reel combination is also essential and there is no combo for all types of waters and situations. Most anglers prefer to use a rod with a fast tip for shaking the lure, and a reel that has a high gear ratio, so that if a bass is in cover, you will be able to get him out quick. Both six foot six and seven foot rods are popular but most pros rely on seven footers. Many rod makers have rods specially designed for Drop-shotting.

When choosing a reel, get one with at least four ball bearings, as this will ensure maximum smoothness. Purchase the best reel that you can afford. Since I backreel and don't rely on the drag at all, it's of no consequence to me. However, if you depend on the drag, make sure the drag is smooth before you purchase the reel.

Just about any small, soft plastic lure will work for drop shot fishing. Keep in mind when choosing your baits that drop-shotting is a finesse tactic and that low impact colors that don't stand out from their surroundings, or aren't likely to alarm or intimidate the bass, are the most logical choices. On the waters that I fish, watermelon or green pumpkin are good colors. As far as the style of bait goes, my favorites are a four inch Weenie worm and a Case four inch drop shot worm. Through trial and error you will be able to find the right bait that mimics the baitfish on your favorite water.

One key aspect to drop-shotting is the length of the leader or line that extends below the hook to which the weight is attached. When fishing rock or mud banks, anywhere from 6 to 18 inches of leader is appropriate. If you are fishing a lake with lots of weeds or deep grass make the leader long enough so the worm is above the weeds and the bass can see it. By dancing a worm over the weeds you give the bass an irresistible offering.

Drop-shotting is very effective on deep, suspended smallmouth. If you locate a school of bass suspended on deep structure with your electronics, position the boat over or near them and drop the bait right on top of them. Shake the worm while keeping the weight on the bottom, use some long pauses and work the area carefully. When dealing with suspended fish you will need to pay extra attention to the length of the leader and you will need to change your leader length throughout the day.

Fishing For Smallmouth Bass

Some anglers have trouble comprehending that they are fishing when the line is slack. The sooner they understand this concept the more fish they will catch. As you move the rig along the bottom letting the line go slack between your shaking, and before feeling the weight on the rod tip, you have to anticipate a strike. Every time you move the sinker ever so slightly, look for any line movement. If you sense something, stop and work the bait in place as long as you can.

I have learned a few ways to fine tune drop shot techniques on the clear water northern lakes that I fish. Many of these lakes also have trout that suspend at all different levels in the water column. The smallmouth suspend off the bottom and can be very tough to catch. While drop-shotting is very effective, on many occasions if everything is not right it won't catch fish. When smallmouth are suspending off the bottom set the drop shot leader a bit longer. This will enable you to jiggle your worm just above the smallmouth. It is important to always place the bait right above suspended fish, because they tend to feed upwards.

Prior to drop-shotting I had one lake where I would just hammer the smallmouth in the spring, but after spawning I could not catch them with anything but leeches. I would drift the leeches in 20 to 25 feet of water and catch lots of smallmouth. I would occasionally catch them with plastics but if I was guiding it got to the point that all I would bring along was a bucket full of leeches.

This was one of the first lakes where I experimented with drop shotting. The night before I was going to take a few clients to the lake I rigged up a drop shot rig on one of my rods. My plan was to wait until my clients had caught a bunch of smallmouth with leeches and then pull out the drop shot rig to see what would happen. I was really desperate to figure out a way to catch summer smallmouth on this lake without using leeches.

Well, everything was going just fine since my clients were catching a lot of smallmouth; in fact, if anything they were catching too many since I was running out of leeches and it was only lunch time. The fact that I had never used the drop shot technique before made me doubtful that I would be making expert drop-shotter's out of my clients. I was just happy that they had caught over 75 smallmouth on leeches even though the leech pile was running low.

I pulled out the six foot six rod with the drop shot rig out of my rod storage and looked through my plastics for a small finesse worm. Keep in mind that this was in 1999 and not many anglers knew about this magical technique. One of my clients looked at my rod and inquired as to my experience with drop-shotting. Never being a very good liar, I said that I had never tried it but since every bass magazine was exploiting this new technique I decided to give it a try.

I told my client that I did not have much for weights but I had a lot of small plastics that would work. My client said, "I have a box full of weights, hooks and plastics. I spent two days this winter fishing with a guide in California who was an expert at drop-shotting."

Never being one to claim to know everything about fishing, I replied, "Talk to me!"

As we drifted across the lake my client showed me how the California guide rigged up his rod and even gave me some of the four inch worms that they had used to catch largemouth bass. After my client rigged up his rod and I rigged up mine we motored back to the suspended smallmouth. The other guy in the boat decided to keep using leeches since we did have a few left and, after all, they were catching fish.

There was a light chop on the water and I positioned my boat effortlessly over the smallmouth that were suspended two feet off the bottom. I decided to just sit back and watch my client since he had done this before. I opted to watch and learn. Yes, I could have played the "know it all" card and just started pretending to be an expert on a subject I knew nothing about but I had too much common sense. After all, I wanted to see this drop shot technique catch fish.

It took a while but eventually my client swept his rod and it became evident that he had caught a smallmouth. After he caught his second smallmouth it was time to give it a try. Due to my seven foot quality rod I could feel the weight on the bottom. It took a few weird movements of the line but I caught my first drop shot smallmouth. My client caught more smallmouth than I did that day but I was happy to see him catching fish and grateful for his willingness to share his expertise with me. By the way, his friend continued to catch smallmouth the rest of the day with leeches.

It was an interesting day on the water. The only thing we were doing differently was we were using monofilament line, which has a lot of stretch. Since I had done my share of walleye fishing using a lighter hook set this was no problem. We were also using a similar hookset that we used when a smallmouth would hit a leech. At that time I had never had any experience with fluorocarbon line. That would soon change as I continued to experiment with drop-shotting. I guess that under certain circumstances a guide can learn a few things from a client!

By adding drop-shotting to my arsenal, not only could I add this lake to the list of summer smallmouth waters but I was able to add a few others as well. The only complaint that I had with the technique was I wondered why I hadn't thought of doing this.

On my day off I will often head for a new lake. By fishing a new lake I will often be able to add the lake to my guide list, but it is also a challenge. On one late June day I decided to head into Michigan and fish a 300 acre clear water lake. I knew the lake had both largemouth and smallmouth bass present but I did not know which bass was the dominate specie.

After launching the boat I do what I always do on a new lake, idle and watch the locator. I idled around the lake and could not mark any structure let alone fish. Finally, I came across a shoreline point. The point was in about 30 feet of water and dropped sharply to a depth of 50 feet. One side of the point dropped sharply and the other side of the point was tapered with scattered areas of gravel mixed with large boulders.

As I watched my electronics I was marking fish suspending about one foot above the boulders in 30 feet of water. The first thing I did was drop out a few floating markers over the boulders that held fish. I was excited and I was hoping that these fish were smallmouth and not walleyes. Not that I have anything against walleyes but I didn't have any live bait with me and I doubted my plastics would catch them.

I was certain that this was an ideal drop shot situation. I positioned the boat perpendicular to the point and the rocks and pointed into the wind. It is important to keep the boat pointing into the wind as this allows you to control the speed of your drift and keep the bait in the strike zone longer. I dropped the drop shot rig with a watermelon four inch finesse worm and allowed it to sink to the bottom. Once it hit bottom I let it sit several seconds and then gave the rod a few twitches. Once I got the rhythm I started to catch smallmouth. I repeated this procedure around the other rocks and again had satisfactory results. If I hadn't used the drop shot technique I may not have caught any fish that day and might have never returned.

Using the right hookset is also of great importance. Many anglers prefer the "reel set" to set the hook rather than the traditional "rip the lips" hookset. The sharp light wire dropshot hooks will penetrate easily with light pressure and you risk breaking the light line on a heavy bass with a hard hookset. A 'reel set" just means you reel in line as you lift the rod all in one motion, creating a steadily increasing pressure on the point of the hook instead of quick, sharp, line snapping jerks. If you buy cheap equipment you will be sorry since you will probably end up with a broken rod.

Drop-shotting is not just a vertical presentation. A **horizontal presentation** involves "dragging" the rig along the bottom. Any time you want to add action to your bait while working it just off the bottom a drop shot is a great choice. The rig is usually flipped or pitched 15-25´ to the target letting the rig drop to the bottom. After jiggling the bait in place on a semi-taunt line, you then slowly drag the rig closer to your boat a foot or two at a time. This seems to work well on largemouth bass that are less active.

Another horizontal drop-shot technique that worked well for me on a 125 acre lake that I fish is to allow your line to go slack after moving the rig forward and jiggling the bait on this slack line for a few seconds. Then weight the line, that is, tighten up on the line to see if you feel anything different. If you do, then set the hook. If not, lift the sinker and move the rig a bit closer repeating the process. I don't know why, but while it works on this lake I have not caught a bass on other lakes using this technique.

If I am fishing a lake that has big smallmouth I will try some creature baits, like a brush hawg. The wider profile of the creature bait will attract larger than average smallmouth and trigger vicious strikes. You will need to tie a wide gap hook onto the drop shot rig. I usually start out with a smaller finesse bait and switch to a creature bait one I have established the bite. Green pumpkin and watermelon are my favorite colors in clear water.

While I use my share of plastics, being a guide it is no secret that when things are tough I switch to live bait. I also deal with families and when you have a couple of young kids in the boat drop shotting in deep water is not an option. However, if the fish are in deep water you need to make an adjustment. On more than one occasion when fishing a clear water smallmouth bait, modifying a drop shot rig with a live leech was a life saver.

I have also modified the drop shot rig for fishing with kids for river smallmouth. When I spend time on the river with kids in summer, it comforts me to know that river smallmouth like to eat nightcrawlers. My typical pattern is to find some rocks that I know are loaded with crayfish that will attract a bunch of hungry smallmouth. Even under the toughest conditions I can produce smallmouth for my clients.

For a lot of years the problem was not in locating smallmouth but figuring out how my young client with little or no experience could catch a smallmouth before they became snagged in the rocks. After trial and error, without realizing it I had developed a modified drop shot rig.

What I would do is tie a Palomar knot with a number four Eagle Claw live bait hook which has barbs on the shank. I would leave a tag line about 12-14 inches long and tie an overhand knot up about three inches from the end of the tag line. Next pinch a slip shot weight above the overhand knot.

Fishing For Smallmouth Bass

To complete the rig I would hook a healthy nightcrawler either through the nose or the middle of the crawler. I found out hooking the crawler in the middle works best for kids since they don't throw the crawler off on the cast, at least most of the time.

The rig can be either set in a rod holder or fished with a slow retrieve. The knot on the end of the tag line helps keep the split shot on. If the rig gets hung up in the rocks the spilt shot breaks off and the split shot can be easily replaced. It is much easier to pinch on a cheap split shot than keep replacing hooks. This rig also tends to allow the crawler to ride a few inches off the bottom triggering more strikes.

I have also had good results with this rig using grubs and plastic worms when smallmouth were holding in six to eight feet of water. I cast the rig upstream and, holding my rod tip high, try to keep as much contact with the bottom as possible. You will need to experiment with different split shots until you find the right weight. If you get snagged up in the rocks, no big deal since all you need to do is replace the split shot.

This can be a deadly presentation if smallmouth are holding tight to rock in heavy current. There are days when dragging a tube just does not get the job done. Instead of using one large split shot I will clinch on three or four in a series. This seems to slide over the rocks easier than one big weight. I cast the rig with a three or four inch curly tail grub perpendicular to the boat with the boat anchored and use a slow steady retrieve.

Drop-shotting has proven to be effective by thousands of anglers all around the globe. It is considered a finesse technique involving light line, light weights and small plastic baits. Whether anglers are fishing in highly pressured waters or remote Canadian Shield lakes, when the fishing gets tough drop-shotting will put more fish in the boat. It should be a tactic in every bass anglers' bag of tricks.

During the late fall period when the water temperature drops below 45 degrees, clear water lakes produce big smallmouth. These big fish can be elusive if not impossible to catch on some lakes in summer and early fall. By late fall the forage base is depleted and it is trophy time. Darker and moderately fertile lakes will have a greater abundance of forage and large predator fish are less apt to cooperate in cold water. Flowages, which are steady producers most of the year, see only fair late fall action although rivers are productive right through ice-up.

The first type of structure I search out is rocks. By November, weeds are dead and don't play an important part in fish location. The last remaining forage can be found relating to rock. By rocks I am referring to both offshore structure and shoreline rocks. These same areas may only hold a few transient fish throughout summer and early fall. On certain days you will find fish relating to the rocks but they don't hold there for extended periods of time. Basically, they move in and out. Once the temperature drops below 48 degrees more and more forage fish move into the rocks. Since all types of forage fish move into the rocks, expect all types of predator fish to be present. Walleye, musky, smallmouth, largemouth and pike may all be present on the same structure. Not only will you find an abundance of fish, but trophy fish as well.

A lake does not have to have an abundance of rock to be productive. If too much rock is present in the lake finding fish can be difficult. Look for lakes with only a few rock piles or rocky points. A fisherman must also understand that all rocks are different. Your favorite rock shoreline that held fish in spring might not be productive in November. However, on other lakes the same rock shoreline can be productive. Rock shorelines with access to deep water are most productive. Shallow rock flats are only productive if they are the only rock available within the lake.

Smallmouth bass tend to school up heavily in November as they relate to deep rocks. Once they are found, the fishing can be fantastic, since they school up according to size. Even the smallest rock point or hump can hold a number of big smallmouth. Big smallmouth will suspend off the rocks and are easy to locate with your electronics. Look for smallmouth to relate to the 20 to 25 foot depths. Once these smallmouth are found, position your boat over the fish. If the wind is strong, anchor your boat upwind which will allow you to cast to the marked fish. The most productive method is to position your boat over the fish with your electric trolling motor. Hold atop the fish and vertical jig. I use both live and artificial bait presentations and the wise fisherman will also use both methods. A jig and chub combo is hard for any hawg smallmouth to pass up. If the bite is light use an Aberdeen hook with a small split shot about 12 inches above the chub. Plastics are also effective but a slow retrieve is a must.

Clear lake smallmouth will also suspend over open water at various depths in the water column as they chase schools of baitfish. Unlike in summer when these suspended smallmouth can have lockjaw, fall fish are very aggressive. Once you locate a school of suspending smallmouth with your electronics, cast a crankbait that will get to the desired depth that imitates the baitfish. Hold on tight to your rod because strikes can be bone shaking since the competition is fierce between these hungry smallmouth. Use a crankbait that best resembles the dominate forage in the lake.

Fishing For Smallmouth Bass

Although these big smallmouth hit the crankbait like a freight train they can be selective, so expect to experiment with color and the speed of your retrieve. Remember that when you catch one fish in the late fall others are present. Making minor adjustments will make the difference from a great day on the water to only catching a few fish.

On many occasions after an angler catches a half dozen smallmouth with a crankbait the bite slows down and no adjustment will work. That is when I grab my other rod rigged with a four or five inch Zipper Grub. The 3-1/2 inch Zipper Grub will keep the action going and could eventually trigger the big fish of the day. Use a slow steady retrieve and, when you feel a strike, wait a few seconds before setting the hook. The colder the water, the slower the retrieve should be.

Fall Football

Jigging spoons are another option and when in the proper hands they will catch lots of big fall smallmouth. Most smallmouth anglers have a love-hate relationship with jigging spoons. To effectively put fish in the boat with a jigging spoon you will need to do everything just right, but if you put in your time you will catch behemoth fall smallmouth. I have caught smallmouth with jigging spoons in stained water lakes, reservoirs and rivers, but they tend to be most effective in clear water.

Having a good success rate with jigging spoons has as much to do with proper rigging as using the proper technique. Most importantly, you need to add a ball bearing swivel to the front of the spoon. This alone will make the difference between a successful outing and a disastrous experience. Spoons are designed to wobble and twist and if you don't add a quality swivel your line will be twisted and you will revert to another presentation after the first 15 minutes.

I again stress "quality" when choosing your swivel. I have tried to add cheaper swivels to the front of my spoons, but have found them not nearly as effective as their higher priced cousins. You will also need to add a split ring to the swivel as you place it on the eye of the spoon. Again, the more expensive stainless steel split rings work best. Brass split rings will work almost as well. I suggest using the smallest swivel and split ring you can find. Avoid snap swivels. There is just too much hardware that hangs up off the top of your bait. The less hardware the less likely it is that the spoon will foul up your line as you jig it up and down in the water column or bounce it off the bottom.

Another important modification is to upgrade the factory provided hooks to premium grade treble hooks. This is important because many strikes come as the spoon is falling. If you use the factory provided hooks (most of them are cheaper dull hooks) you will lose fish. I personally use a #2 or #4 Gamakatsu treble hook depending on the size of the spoon. Be sure you have extra hooks with you as you leave the ramp in the morning. I will often change hooks during the day to ensure that I won't miss fish. If you are jigging on the bottom or bouncing off rocks even a top quality hook will dull. Along with the hook make sure you have a set of split ring pliers in the boat. It beats jabbing either your thumb nail or another hook point into the split ring as you attempt to change the hook. Ouch!

As far as the spoon itself my favorite is the legendary Hopkins Shorty 75. This spoon weighs 3/4 ounce and I find that it will work for the majority of jigging spoon applications. Another favorite spoon, especially on windy days, is the 1 ounce Mega Bass. The spoon has a slimmer profile and is less apt to give you wider "fluttering" action than the Hopkins does, allowing you to keep in contact with the bait when fighting the wind. As far as colors of spoons, I prefer to use the most natural colors possible. This means a polished and hammered nickel finish.

Now for the technique: Most of my clear water spoon fishing revolves around the presence of baitfish. In fall, big smallmouth are more likely to

Fishing For Smallmouth Bass

follow schools of baitfish than relate to structure. With my electronics I search for schools of baitfish suspending over open water or off structure; the larger the school of baitfish the better. Once a school of baitfish is located, I drop the spoon straight down to the desired depth and hop it up and down (like a yo-yo) on a relatively tight line just under the school. Be sure to keep in contact with the spoon, since better than half of the strikes come as the bait is falling. Once you feel the spoon stop falling or a sudden "thump" as you snap the bait upwards, quickly set the hook.

Quality electronics are a must. Crank up the sensitivity so that you can get the best possible picture on your unit. Also keep in mind that you may have to re-adjust your unit throughout the day. The high adjustments you made while you are looking for baitfish will usually scramble your picture once you start moving fast.

Another thing to keep in mind is that it is a necessary evil that the spoon will occasionally hang in the line. The more the boat moves, whether it is from the trolling motor or the wind,
the more often the spoon will foul. Try and keep the boat as still as possible when you begin jigging. Once you feel that you have covered an area sufficiently enough, move the boat on a slow trolling motor speed, or allow the boat to drift slowly with the wind. Trust me, the spoon will occasionally foul. It's not that you are doing something wrong, or that your spoon is not working properly. I typically find that the more slack that I snap into the line on the yo-yo, the more often the spoon fouls. Keep the line tight both on the way up and down to reduce this nuisance.

When fishing jigging spoons, there is no place for a finesse rod with a fast tip. I prefer a 6' 6" medium heavy baitcasting rod spooled with 10 pound test fluorocarbon line for 3/4 and one ounce spoons. If the action is slow I will switch to smaller 1/8 to 1/2 ounce spoons. I prefer a 6' 6" medium heavy spinning rod and spool my reel with 8 pound fluorocarbon line for these lighter spoons.

At first glance blade baits resemble jigging spoons. While they can in fact be used for vertical jigging they are best used with a cast and retrieve presentation. Like jigging spoons they will catch smallmouth in stained water but they shine in clear water.

My favorite blade bait is the Silver Buddy. It was designed by Buddy Banks and Billy Westmoreland. Billy and Buddy worked for a long time to perfect the balance between lead and aluminum. Billy Westmoreland once called the Silver Buddy the best lure ever to catch smallmouth bass.

I have had great success fishing the Silver Buddy when smallmouth are feeding on suspended bait fish. All you need to do is cast the Silver Buddy targeting the baitfish. Next, count the bait down about a foot per second, then raise and lower the bait, reeling up the slack and keeping a semi-tight line. This method will keep the bait in the strike zone and you can vary your count until you connect with the fish. Due to its weight and compact size you are able to cast the Silver buddy a mile making it ideal on those cold front days common in the fall.

Blade baits can also be jigged off of the bottom. I like to cast it out and let it fall all the way to the bottom. Then I lift it up three or four feet and let it fall back to the bottom again. Your strikes are going to come on the fall, so you need to let the lure fall on a semi-tight line. If you don't, you won't feel the little "tick" that indicates a strike. Sometimes you will want a slow, short hop and sometimes they want you to rip the bait five or six feet off the bottom. You just need to experiment until you figure out the bite for the day.

When fishing the Silver Buddy I use a six foot six medium heavy action spinning rod and spool my reel with eight or ten pound monofilament. Why do I use heavy line in clear water? Well, anytime you throw a bait with treble hooks and let it drop on the bottom you are going to get hung up occasionally. If you are using six or eight pound test you can plan on using lots of lures.

Catching smallmouth in clear water lakes is a lot of fun and very challenging. At times the fishing can seem easy, but most of the time, you will need to rely on finesse presentations. Be prepared to adjust to the conditions.

Chapter 9
Fall River Patterns

Weeds are first on my list during the fall. Even though weeds can hold smallmouth in summer, the bite can be unpredictable. One day you will find active smallmouth and the next day there isn't a fish to be found. This unpredictable bite is due to the forage. In summer, food is plentiful and schools of baitfish will migrate as they feed on a variety of smaller baitfish, insect larva and plankton. Basically, smallmouth are just following the food chain.

The key to the weed smallmouth river bite is a major drop in the water temperature. Cool nights can cause a sharp drop in the water temperature. This drop in the water temperature will push scattered baitfish out of the decaying weeds and they will school up along the weedline. On a cool crisp frosty fall morning it is not unusual to connect with a load of spirited bronzebacks foraging on an easy meal.

Several presentations are effective but topwater baits are my first choice, and being a topwater aficionado I never miss out on an opportunity. The topwater bite can also be incredible. As a guide I dream of these situations, for I have yet to encounter a client who is not quick to tie on a topwater bait. If the water temperature rises later in the day, the topwater bite will continue but smallmouth will start to roam the weedline making the topwater bite less effective. If the water temperature does not rise smallmouth will remain bunched up.

Although the topwater bite can be explosive the catching will take patience. The trick is to cover water effectively. If I don't get a quick response with the topwater lure, I will have one of my clients switch to a spinnerbait. The spinnerbait is a better search bait and enable the angler to make faster casts. Once you stick a fish with either bait, continue to use both baits until you determine that there is a definite topwater bite.

Prop baits work best when fishing weedlines. Prop baits create more commotion and better resemble surfacing baitfish. Occasionally, I will cast a popper and if the smallmouth are in a more neutral mood it will be the ticket. If you are on big fish water then try giving the four inch Hubs Chub a try. The four inch Hubs Chub will produce plenty of big fall smallmouth on all types of water but it is particularly effective in rivers. If there is a chop on the water, walking the dog is the preferred presentation. If you are confronted with calm conditions or a slight ripple on the water, I prefer to pop the Hubs Chub. I have caught smallmouth on both the three inch and four inch Hubs Chub with water temperatures as low as 45 degrees.

The Smithwick Devil's Horse excels for big fall smallmouth when fishing weeds. As with all surface baits, try to cast in the vicinity of surfacing baitfish. My favorite presentation is the same technique that worked on my first successful outing. Cast the bait and wait a few seconds after the lure hits the water. Next, start to pop and buzz the bait making lots of commotion. The only problem when fishing low light periods is the bite off by northern pike and muskies. Due to the stainless steel wire running through the lure it can withstand an attack by a toothy critter, although you might need to re-adjust the props.

Another deadly tactic is to use the Devils Horse both as a surface bait and as a shallow running stickbait. Make your cast at shoreline cover, give it a few twitches and then retrieve it back to the boat. This will make the lure dive down to about four feet. Another option is to use a stop and go approach. To do this, crank the lure to get it to the desired depth, then stop. Let it float back up to the top, give it a few twitches and again start your retrieve. Experiment with different retrieves and you might be surprised with your results.

The Zara Spook is a bait that I seldom use when guiding, but on occasion I will spend time coaching a client on how to walk-the-dog. While some anglers catch on quickly it is an ordeal for most of my clients. The problem is that if they do get the rhythm going and catch a fish or two, if they don't keep refining the presentation they will quickly lose the rhythm. Many of my clients bring along a Spook and if the time is right I will encourage them to give it a try. If it is in the hands of a competent angler it is a wonderful lure to watch, especially when a big smallmouth crushes it. And, it is an awesome bait for big fall smallmouth.

It is common to hook two smallmouth on one topwater lure. In fact, on one occasion I was fishing along and, looking for big smallmouth decided to throw a Zara Super Spook with three treble hooks. I had made several casts without a short strike or even what I could confirm was a follow. While getting ready to change to another surface bait I saw a bunch of baitfish flying out of the water. I put the trolling motor on high and headed directly to the source of all the commotion.

It was an easy cast since there were still riffles on the surface. It seemed as if the water exploded before the giant spook hit the water. I set the hook and literally could not move whatever I had hooked. At first I thought I was either hung up in the weeds or hooked a big pike or muskie. However, it did not take long for me to realize that it was no pike but two nice smallmouth both having different thoughts about the direction they should take. I was making steady progress when my bait came to an abrupt halt. This lasted a few seconds before the surface again exploded and the fight became more intense. Things were getting pretty dismal and for a while I could not make any progress. Finally I began gaining ground but was in total shock when I scooped three smallmouth into the boat. That was the easy part, now I had to untangle three smallmouth, and three extra sharp treble hooks.

So that is my all time smallmouth record; three 18 inch smallmouth with one cast. It's a feat I am sure I will never duplicate. It's a good thing I had my casting rod with braided line for I don't think my other casting rod with 12 pound fluorocarbon could have done the trick.

Although the topwater bite is great, a spinnerbait will consistently catch fall smallmouth in rivers and reservoirs. The advantage of a spinnerbait is whether you are fishing weeds or shoreline cover they are easy to use even for inexperienced anglers. That said, besides being user friendly they produce big fall smallmouth. I wish I could use them more in the summer when fishing the river but they are seldom the most effective lure.

While they are user friendly it is a common mistake for anglers to chuck the spinnerbait as far as they can chuck it and retrieve it back to the boat ignoring the action of the lure. Normally I will not simply retrieve a spinnerbait back to the boat without some sort of variation in my retrieve. Smallmouth have a tendency to follow a spinnerbait back to the boat. If I notice that a straight retrieve will not draw strikes, I give the rod tip a sharp and powerful twitch, usually a few times during the retrieve but while reeling steady. The sudden change in the retrieve will trigger a strike. The twitch breaks the monotonous single action of the bait for a split second which breaks the fish's stare at a boring and unnatural single action bait.

Even if a fish is not hungry or even stuffed, it will still react to this type of maneuver (by bait or live prey) like you do when a doctor taps your nerve during a physical, because Mother Nature has programmed that fish to do that. It is a natural reaction to help the fish to stay alive, by eating what it can when any opportunity, especially an easy one, presents itself. Essentially, you're trying to convince the fish that the spinnerbait is a real food item. If you have already determined the proper color, blade(s) and head sizes based on the dominant forage, it's size, weather, time of year, type of fishery, and the hundred gazillion other factors affecting your choices, then the one remaining factor to consider is that boring single action style retrieve. Add in a little twitch to your retrieve and see what happens.

Another factor to consider is color. I tend to rely on more solid skirt hues and gold blades when fishing stained water rivers. Many times a slight color change may be all that is needed to convince a following, hesitant fish to strike. I will normally make subtle color changes, say from a bait with a clear/gold metalflake skirt to a similar one with green added, or from an all white bait to a white bait with a little chartreuse until I find the best bite, but I will not hesitate to switch to a color on the other end of the spectrum. Smallmouth are difficult fish to catch consistently as they do not like to adhere to a set of rules like largemouth will do.

When water temperatures reach the 40s, it's time to slow-roll larger spinnerbaits in slightly deeper water areas nearby to wintering haunts. Bass are now searching for larger meals for which they don't have to work as hard to capture. Slowly reeling the spinnerbait, and almost never with a straight retrieve but with pauses and light twitches so that it ticks off boulders, wood and other bottom cover, will entice strikes from more

Fishing For Smallmouth Bass

lethargic bass.

What type of rod works best for fishing spinnerbaits? With a spinnerbait, you are talking about a reaction-type bait. You want the rod to let the bait work. Too many times guys will try to get one rod to work everything. When you use one rod to fish topwater baits, crankbaits, worms and jigs, what you are doing is compromising. Fiberglass works well because the softer action of most fiberglass rods allows the spinnerbait to work as they are designed. Some graphite rods work for throwing spinnerbaits, but they need to have softer action. A fast-action rod won't allow the bait to work right.

It can be challenging to choose an ideal length for a spinnerbait rod. The length depends on several factors, including each person's casting style and height. For the most part, anglers use a 6 1/2- to 7-foot rod.

Crankbaits will catch summer smallmouth relating to rocks and current and they are a great lure to use when searching for active fish. However, on most days soft plastics or a topwater lure will be the most productive. I only occasionally use crankbaits when fishing reservoirs in summer and that is usually on a day when I have trouble locating fish. The problem is that in the summer you will pick up an occasional scattered fish and can't develop a pattern. You can get your hopes up after sticking a big fish but you need to keep on the move. On such days a crankbait is the bait of choice.

As the water temperature drops in fall, both river and reservoir smallmouth will show a preference for crankbaits. The good news is that the drop in water temperature causes smallmouth to school up, and when you connect with a big smallmouth on a crankbait you are almost certain to catch more.

Even if you have a good topwater or spinnerbait bite it is a smart idea to follow up with a crankbait before moving to another area, especially if you caught a few big fish. After you catch a few fish the rest of the smallmouth can drop down deeper into the water column and refuse to rise up to hit a topwater or spinner type bait. The advantage to fishing with a crankbait when you are fishing a weedline is that you are able to cover the entire water column. Start out with a mid-depth running crankbait and next move to a deep diver.

The type of crankbait I use depends on both the water temperature and the preferred forage. In the early fall I use almost exclusively wide wobbling plastic crankbaits with rattle inserts. The rattle will both trigger a strike and attract a smallmouth from a greater distance. Once the water temperature drops below 50 degrees I switch to a crankbait with a tighter action and by the time the temperature drops below 40 degrees I switch to wood crankbaits. Most wood crankbaits have a tight action and are more buoyant. When retrieving a wood crankbait I use a slow steady retrieve with an occasional pause. On the pause the buoyancy of the wood crankbait allows the bait to rise slowly which will trigger a strike in the cold water.

Smallmouth will still forage on crayfish in the fall but for the most part it is a minnow bite. On most of the stained water rivers and reservoirs that I fish, shiners and chubs are the main fall forage so I match my crankbaits accordingly. Silver/black, white, chartreuse/white and fire tiger patterns work best. Like any other lure don't get locked into one color pattern. When the bite is tough don't be afraid to experiment.

Most of my crankbait fishing is done with a bait casting reel since I feel I have greater control over the action of the crankbait, especially when using larger cranks. If I am using smaller bait I opt for a spinning set up which allows me to cast farther and cover more water. A good crankbait rod should be either six foot six or seven feet long and have medium light power. The main reason for employing medium-light power is the positive reaction of the rod when retrieving cranks. Resistance from the bill of the crank loads the rod almost half way, leaving little bend to remove on the hookset while leaving a smallmouth little chance to relieve pressure once it touches the point of a hook.

On some days, smallmouth prefer a measured presentation and a spinnerbait or crankbait won't get the job done. That is why I carry a good supply of soft plastic jerkbaits. Twitching a soft plastic jerkbait in shallow weeds can trigger strikes when all else seems to fail. They are also a follow up bait after you have caught several smallmouth with a topwater, spinnerbait or crankbait.

Just as when fishing the river grass in summer, it is important to fish both the weeds and the weed line. The Case Sinking Shad is my favorite fall bait for weed related smallmouth and largemouth bass. When fishing weeds I will work the Sinking Shad at a moderate speed looking for aggressive bass. When working the weedline, I work the jerkbait slowly and let it drop along the weedline. I catch big bass with both presentations.

Imitating the preferred forage is important. Fishing a soft plastic jerkbait along the edge of a creek channel or slough is the best way that I know to imitate a live red tail chub or shiner. Make sure you effectively fish the area by working the top and mid sections of the water column. Cast the jerkbait rigged with a 4/0 wide gap hook right on the edge of the creek channel and close to weeds. Once the bait hits the surface I will give it a vigorous twitch then reel up the slack as quickly as possible in anticipation of a savage strike. If a bass does not inhale the jerkbait, give it another twitch and let it sink along the edge of the weeds. Then after about five seconds give it a few short twitches making sure your line is taught. Watch your line since a big smallmouth will head for deep water. If you see your line moving toward deep water reel in the slack before setting the hook.

Both these smallmouth hit a Case Sinking Shad

On one cold October day my clients and I caught a load of big smallmouth on the edge of a small creek. It was one of those days when after a few hours of short strikes and missed fish I knew my clients would be happy if they caught a few 18 inch smallmouth. Making matters worse, I was unable to get my hands on any red tail chubs or any other usable minnows. So I headed up-river to one of my favorite holes, but without any minnows on this cold front day I had low expectations.

I positioned my boat downstream from the slough and the creek channel, dropped the trolling motor and instructed the client in the front of the boat to cast a spinnerbait and the guy in the back to cast a Case sinking Shad. The guy with the spinnerbait did not get a strike as he worked the bait over the weeds. However, the results were different with the guy casting the soft plastic jerkbait. On his third cast he yelled "Fish on" and I responded by netting a 19 inch smallmouth.

Usually after one of my clients catches a big fish I don't have the other client switch immediately but under these conditions I told him to make a change. We spent the next 45 minutes moving back and forth along the creek channel, ultimately catching 20 smallmouth without so much as one being under 18 inches. We made a few stops at other spots but returned a few hours later and caught another dozen smallmouth with soft plastic jerkbaits. It was truly another great day on the river.

As far as color goes, I seldom use a jerkbait that does not imitate a baitfish. Look into my bag of tricks and you will find white, pearl, and white with silver and gold flakes. On occasion I will throw a natural colored bait like green pumpkin or watermelon on a clear water lake. When fishing deep clear water lakes it is important to use fluorocarbon line, which will allow the jerkbait to sink to its maximum depth.

One issue some have with soft plastic jerkbaits is that they have trouble setting the hook. This is a result of the angler's poor choice of rod as opposed to their technique. Most anglers who complain about losing fish are usually using a light action rod with a fast tip. Anglers who have success fishing jerkbaits prefer a six foot six or seven foot medium heavy rod with a lot of backbone and spool their reels with braided line to eliminate stretch. This set up works in most types of water.

When fishing on the river for smallmouth and I am using a four inch jerkbait, I like to use a six foot six medium action spinning rod spooled with eight pound fluorocarbon/monofilament Hybrid line. When using five inch jerkbaits I use a bait caster but my choice of line will depend on how far in the water column I want the jerkbait to fall. By using 10 pound fluorocarbon line the jerkbait can be fished as deep as ten feet. If I am fishing over grass I will spool my baitcaster with braided line. So as with any plastic bait, your choice in line will be dictated by the type of cover and water depth.

Few things in fishing can be guaranteed, but when the water temperature is 50 degrees, find a bend in the river, an incoming creek, and a deep hole and you will find monster smallmouth. Areas like this have enabled me to put big smallmouth in the boat for my clients on both an annual and daily basis. The only problem is that it can make fishing look too easy and my client's expectations can be too high.

On occasion you can fish a spot too much. Let's face it-- fishing can only get so good.

Take the time I fished a creek channel with Mike Poja from M i l w a u k e e. Mike, who was well into his 80's, would bring along a friend and they would fish with me for a couple of days. He knew where my hot spots were so it was hard to fish any other places. Many of my clients cherish the spots we fish and the spots where they catch a big fish are as memorable as the fish.

On one particular trip, Mike brought along his son, who had not fished with me before. Over my 25 plus years of guiding I learned to never go to the hot spot right away. We started the day as I often do, fishing secondary spots to get the feel of the day, especially with a new client in the boat. Now, we caught a few nice chunky smallmouth but as I gazed at Mike he was wondering why we were not fishing the creek channel.

Finally, I headed up river to the "Hot Spot". Since I had not fished the creek channel for a few days I was very confident that big smallmouth would be present. I cautiously moved into the edge of the creek and eased the anchor into the river. The boat was positioned perfectly, leaving my clients within casting distance right where the creek entered the river. Positioning the boat in the right area is extremely critical for catching big smallmouth.

Mike made a cast with a red tail chub and as soon as the chub hit the water a behemoth smallmouth engulfed it. We soon boated a six pound 21 inch smallmouth. After a few photos the smallmouth was released and Mike soon had another smallmouth that easily went over five pounds. His son also managed to catch a five pounder along with several over 18 inches; an excellent day of smallmouth bass fishing in anyone's book.

On the ride to the river the next day we were all reminiscing about the great fishing and the anticipation of more giant smallmouth. Needless to say, it was impossible to avoid going right to the "Hot Spot". Again, with care, I positioned the boat in the perfect location. However, after a few casts we had not even had a bite. Finally, we managed to catch an 18 inch smallmouth that easily pushed four pounds. We continued to work the area, but could not boat a smallmouth over 18 inches.

We fished several other areas and again, nice smallmouth but nothing over 18 inches. While we still had a good day on the water, it was hard to beat the previous day. Mike and his son were pleased but I could sense a bit of disappointment since we did not catch any big smallmouth that day. If only the days had been reversed.... On occasion, that does happen.

Fishing creek channels is great but don't make the mistake of not fishing the surrounding structure. After smallmouth gorge themselves on baitfish they will drop down to the closest available structure and can hold tight for extended periods of time. If you mix in a cold front this structure can be a magnet for huge schools of hungry smallmouth. I found this out the hard way years ago quit accidentally.

While I have had many memorable days on the water those bad weather days stick out in my mind, not just because of the misery but because most often they were learning experiences. These are the kind of days when if I was not fishing for money I would not be on the water. Mix in high water and gale force winds and all your expertise and sanity will be challenged. A little luck will never hurt. If my anchor had not slipped I never would h a v e found that honey hole. By the way, I have been fishing that tree for years and to this day it still produces loads of smallmouth. However, I fish it sparingly and keep it for when the chips are down.

A series of storms made its way through the area and dropped heavy rain raising the water level in the river. Prior to the rain I was pounding smallmouth off the edge of a creek channel. I wanted to make that creek channel my first stop hoping to beat other anglers to the punch. Although with a 30 mph northwest wind I wasn't expecting too much competition.

I approached the creek channel and with the wind and current it was obvious that my trolling motor would be of no use. So I dropped the anchor upstream from the creek and let enough slack out on the anchor line to position the boat so my client could cast into the creek channel. Everything looked great and when my client caught a 16 inch smallmouth on a red tail chub with his first cast things were looking up. However, by the time my client got the smallmouth to the boat the anchor slipped and we were on our way downstream.

I was getting ready to pull up the anchor when the boat came to an abrupt halt almost evicting me from the bow of the boat. Needless to say the anchor found a home. I tried retrieving the anchor and soon realized we found some wood and were hung up in seven feet of water. I told my clients to drop their chubs, which were rigged on 1/0 circle hooks with a small split shot, down to the bottom, hoping to make hay out of a bad situation.

Well, it did not take long for the boat to heat up as both my clients yelled "Fish on." It looked like both clients had hooked big fish and I simultaneously scooped two 19inch smallmouth into the boat. After we took a few photos and released the smallmouth to swim another day the feat was quickly

136

duplicated with the exception being that one of my clients' fish pushed 21 inches. It was as good as it gets. My clients ended up doubling up with big smallmouth on 7 consecutive casts. All good things do come to an end as the action finally slowed and we continued to fish for 20 minutes without a strike.

Bob Galbierz with a smallmouth that was holding on the edge of a creek channel

I decided to make a move possibly to the other end of the wood, but now I had to deal with the anchor. I pulled, yanked, and even tried to use the outboard to loosen the anchor but eventually had to admit defeat. I had no other option but to cut the anchor rope. I had been there before and told my clients not to worry because I had a spare anchor.

Now I had a dilemma: do I tie on my spare anchor and continue to fish the area or do I move to a safer area. I opted to fish a few other spots but unfortunately they did not hold any active smallmouth. So I had no option but to return to that tree and drop down the anchor while carefully trying to avoid a hang up. We did catch a few more fish but I was in no hurry thinking my anchor would again be snagged in the tree. However, this time with a little luck I easily retrieved the anchor.

A little luck will never hurt. If my anchor had not slipped I never would have found that honey hole. The trick to fishing the tree properly is you need to drag the anchor and jar the tree to activate the fish. Always remember to bring along a spare anchor. You can stock a bait shop with the anchors that I have lost in that tree.

River smallmouth relate to mid-river structure in summer and if sufficient forage is present they will remain in the area through the late fall. If only rock is present the food supply will be limited and low to moderate numbers of smallmouth will be present. You will occasionally find fall smallmouth but you will need the combination of grass and rock to attract the mother load. Just like shoreline weeds, mid-river weed action ripens when the water temperature begins to drop and not when the calendar dictates.

Most of the time you will be fishing water that is less than five feet. These grass related smallmouth will jump on a topwater bait but most of the time the grass grows to the surface. You will end up spending more time cleaning grass off the topwater lure than keeping it in the strike zone. The same holds true for shallow running crankbaits; if you can avoid the grass they will catch smallmouth, but that is easier said than done. The only sure bet when choosing an artificial bait is a soft plastic jerkbait rigged Texas style.

In the early fall the grass is high so make sure you use a buoyant jerkbait like a Zoom Fluke. Most of the time you will be fishing water that is less than five feet. The closer you can fish the jerkbait to the surface the more effective it will be. It is not that smallmouth won't hit a sun surface jerkbait, but if the jerkbait sinks too much you will continuously get hung up in the weeds. Later in fall when the grass starts to decay, using a sinking soft plastic jerkbait like a Case Sinking Shad will trigger more strikes.

My choice in line will depend on how deep I want the jerkbait to drop. If I want the jerkbait to ride high I prefer braided line since it floats. If I want the jerkbait to sink I use either fluorocarbon or monofilament line. I use a six foot six medium or medium/heavy action rod and prefer to use a baitcasting reel. A baitcaster allows me to have greater control over the action of the jerkbait.

How you will approach the grass will depend on the current and your boat. The ideal presentation is to use your trolling to move slowly upstream. As you move into the current cast the jerkbait slightly upstream on a 45 degree angle and after the jerkbait hits the water slowly reel up the slack while getting ready to set the hook. If you are asleep at the switch you will miss fish. Just as when fishing a topwater bait make sure you feel the fish

138

on before you set the hook.

If you don't get a strike with the rod pointed towards the water give the bait a few short aggressive twitches and again pause and reel in the slack. I continue to use a variety of fast and slow twitches varying my pause time until I approach the boat. There is no such thing as a perfect way to retrieve a soft plastic jerkbait. The more you vary your retrieve the more fish you will catch. Be alert because some of the largest smallmouth will hit at boat side.

If you can't fish with the boat going into the current than drift with the current but try to slow down the drift as much as possible. As you drift downstream cast downstream at a 45 degree angle and repeat the same retrieve as if you were fishing into the current. If the current is swift you will need to keep on your toes to keep a tight line.

Don't make the mistake of drifting over the grass too fast. Once you connect with a smallmouth, stop the drift and use your electric trolling motor to hold your boat in place. I try to avoid using a conventional anchor in shallow water unless it is my only option. If you do anchor, do so as stealthily as possible, trying not to spook the larger smallmouth.

If the action slows in the grass don't panic because there is no need to pick up the trolling motor and go for a boat ride. Smallmouth will move off the grass flat and drop down to any deeper cover after feeding. If the grass flat is in three or four feet of water then six to eight feet will qualify as deeper water. The best areas will be a combination of boulders and submerged wood which act as a current break. Boulders and wood alone will hold smallmouth but the more elements that are present and the larger the structure the more smallmouth that will be present.

The good thing is that when fall smallmouth drop back down to deeper water they are still active. Even under extreme weather conditions the urge to gorge themselves makes them very vulnerable, unlike summer when you will have at best a 50/50 chance that they will respond. Once you locate a prime deep holding area keep on it since the area will hold smallmouth until ice keeps you off the river.

If you are dealing with adverse weather conditions then live bait might be the most effective presentation. If you are fishing during a severe weather change use a sinking soft plastic jerkbait and start fishing deeper water adjacent to the grass. The first area I look for is boulders and submerged wood.

A medium running crankbait can also be the ticket. The trick is to retrieve the crankbait close to the bottom and when you feel the rocks, jerk the crankbait and let it rise up a few feet. If you don't feel a strike when the crankbait rises continue the retrieve until you bounce off another rock. Suspending jerkbaits are another option.

Soft plastic jerkbaits catch their share of grass related smallmouth but on some days it's hard to beat a red tail chub. One September day I fished with Jamie Trapp and Ed Ruff. It was a foggy morning and I had to go for a boat ride since there was an ex-client parked in my honey hole close to the boat landing. I must admit that over the past ten years this has become a problem for me as clients use my services so they can find a hot spot and then sit on it until they fish it out. Many of them bamboozle me into thinking they are catch and release fisherman but I continuously watch them place 20 inch smallmouth into the live well. These 10-12 year old smallmouth deserve a better destiny than ending up on the edge of a fillet knife. That is why God made walleyes and perch. I guess it is a sign of the times and something I just have to deal with, but I wish these people would think of the longer term impact they are having on the fishery before they eat every smallmouth they catch.

Anyway, after a tricky boat ride in the dense fog, due primarily due to the many dead heads in the river, I approached my favorite fall honey hole. I dropped the trolling motor and told Jamie and Ed to cast their red tail chubs to the right. As soon as the chub hit the water Jamie had a smallmouth breaking water and within a few seconds, Ed also acknowledged that he also had a fish on. This was the start of a great day on the water.

After we boated a bunch of nice fish I explained to Jamie and Ed why this spot held so many smallmouth. I pointed out that there is a mid-river ridge that runs down the center of the river. On the outer edge of the ridge the rocks drop from four to eight feet. Grass is abundant on the shallow part of the ridge which attracts a variety of baitfish making it an ideal feeding area. On the deep edge of the ridge, boulders break the current and attract non-feeding smallmouth. I told my clients that this makes for ideal habitat that will hold large numbers of smallmouth through ice up. It took me a while to explain this to my clients since they kept interrupting me with the fish they were catching.

I fish several areas like this on the Menominee River and year after year they consistently produce for me. If forage is abundant they attract smallmouth and if forage is limited smallmouth are still attracted to the area. In seven hours we boated over 60 smallmouth with about 50 percent of the fish measuring between 18 to 20 inches. Now that is fantastic smallmouth fishing in anyone's book. After we ran out of chubs we continued to catch a bunch of smallmouth with Case Sinking Shads.

A few weeks later my friend Mike Jackson returned to the Menominee River to do a story for the Daily Herald, a suburban Chicago newspaper. Mike brought along a few friends, Ken Kortas and Jerry Hermes. Since we needed two boats my friend Bob Dekker helped me out. We had three days of phenomenal smallmouth fishing. We fished two different stretches of the river with both soft plastic jerkbaits and red tail chubs and the results were the same, lots of smallmouth and they were big. Mike Jackson boated the biggest smallmouth of the trip, a massive 22 incher that was easily six pounds and both Ken and Jerry landed their share of lunkers.

By late October when the water temperature drops into the mid-forties we might put a few less numbers of smallmouth in the boat but we catch a higher percentage of trophies. In fact, it is the norm that we boat smallmouth over 20 inches each day. George Luvisi and his friend Barb made their annual trip up north and fished a few days with me on the Menominee River. As usual the weather was cold and the fish were on the feed. George has fished with me for over 20 years and I can count on one hand the number of nice comfortable days we have fished together. The water temperature was in the low 40's and on the ride to the boat landing I told George that the smallmouth were putting on the feed big time. After 2 days of fishing we caught several smallmouth in the 20 inch class with George's big smallmouth of the trip measuring over 21-1/2 inches.

Once of George's favorite places to fish is a stump field on the edge of a shallow bay. The stump field is also adjacent to the main river channel. This puts the stumps out of the main current and smallmouth move into the stumps once the water temperature drops below 50 degrees. I explained to George long ago that once the water temperature drops below 50 degrees the big smallmouth like to find cover out of the current that is close to a food source.

The stump field will produce fine catches of big smallmouth even under the worst weather conditions. The t rick is to position your boat either with the trolling motor or an anchor so my clients can cast soft plastics or red tail chubs towards the stumps and let the bait fall along the edge of the stump. Under adverse weather conditions big smallmouth are hesitant to leave the comforts of the stump. This technique requires a lot of patience, especially with a brisk northwest wind.

Once the water temperature drops below 40 degrees fishing with soft plastics or crankbaits can be tough. As the water temperature continues to drop the less likely smallmouth are to leave the wood cover. When choosing an artificial lure I use either a finesse jig or a tube. Since I could never find the ideal cold water finesse jig for northern smallmouth I developed my own. I use a 1/8 or 1/4 ounce jighead with an oversized elongated hook with a wire weedguard. I tie on a sparse rubber skirt and tip the jig with a Zipper rigged grub. It is extremely deadly when fishing wood in cold water. I will also catch weedline smallmouth throughout the year.

On most days you will score with a finesse jig but on those days when nothing seems to work I pretend I am walleye fishing. I tie on a chartreuse 1/16 or 1/8 ounce leadhead and tip it with a fathead minnow. The smaller fathead minnow is more effective than the larger red tail chubs when water temperatures drop below 40 degrees.

Bridges are famous for attracting big smallmouth and at no time are your odds better for catching a trophy than in the fall. In fact, bridges have salvaged many a guide trip when I was about ready to reach for the dynamite. Not just in the fall, but I always tell anglers that every time they pass a bridge, FISH IT! Migrating smallmouth can move into the area at anytime using it for both a rest area and a restaurant.

The water gauge height and current will play heavily in your decision as to where to start fishing when you approach the bridge. During rising or high water smallmouth will be most active. The increased current will force baitfish to suspend high in the water column or hold tight to the structure of the bridge. The first place to fish would be concrete or rocks on the deepest side of the bridge.

Approach the bridge with caution and look for any signs of surfacing baitfish since this will also signal the activity level of the smallmouth. If you do see surface activity you can expect the action to be hot and heavy. My first choice of bait under these conditions would be a soft plastic jerkbait. Cast the jerkbait as tight as possible to the bridge structure and be prepared for a strike as soon as the jerkbait hits the water. On many occasions I have had smallmouth actually jump out of the water and grab the jerkbait in mid air. When smallmouth are in a feeding frenzy the competition is so fierce that a smallmouth will do anything to beat its adversary. There have been countless days when fishing soft plastic jerkbaits around bridges has resulted in catches of 20 to 30 smallmouth with most of the fish measuring over 18 inches.

After you catch all the active fish or the frenzy comes to a halt I switch to a grub. The grub will enable you to fish all levels of the water column. I use both three or four inch curly tail grubs and Zipper grubs. Start fishing the grub a few feet below the surface with a slow steady retrieve. Let the grub drop one foot deeper into the water column until you connect with smallmouth. Crankbaits can be effective but you won't be able to get the bait down to the desired depth in the water column.

If you are dealing with low water levels and limited current look for the bulk of the smallmouth to be holding deep in the water column. I say deep in the water column because they will not necessarily be holding tight to the bottom. Generally, under low water conditions, smallmouth will be holding within four feet of the bottom. While these fish will not be overly aggressive, like during high water, they are still very catchable.

The best method to catching these deeper smallmouth is with a finesse jig or a tube. Make long casts so you will be able to keep the bait in the strike zone over a longer period of time. Once your jig hits the bottom give it a few hops and drag it a few feet. Keep hopping the jig until you are under the boat. Once the jig is under the boat, jig it vertically for about a minute. The more aggressive retrieve is often needed to trigger a strike.

I have had limited success fishing a drop shot rig if the current is not too swift. This technique can be deadly when smallmouth are suspending one or two feet off the bottom. Even with limited current you will need to add more weight than when fishing a natural lake in order to ensure that the weight remains on the bottom. The drop shot rig is deadly on those days when smallmouth will not chase a horizontal presentation and seem to have lockjaw.

Just like a bridge, deep pools also have the potential to hold giant fall smallmouth. The best holes will have a steep rock ledge on the upstream edge of the hole and also have an ample food source nearby. If the hole does not have available forage smallmouth will hold overnight but continue with their migration the next day. If forage is available they will move out of the hole to feed and move back into the hole.

While these movements can occur at anytime throughout the day, for the most part smallmouth will hunker down in the hole at night and move shallow to feed in early morning. Just as with the bridge a new batch of smallmouth can move into the hole overnight and use it as a motel on their downstream migration.

The first thing I look for when searching for active smallmouth is a combination of rock and grass along the shoreline. This combination will attract baitfish and the area becomes a prime smallmouth feeding area. Casting shallow or mid-depth crankbaits is the best presentation to connect with actively feeding smallmouth. My second choice of lure would be a soft plastic jerkbait. Use both presentations and you will be able to catch both the aggressive and neutral smallmouth. If heavy weed growth is present then use a spinnerbait.

If you fish a shoreline and don't see any signs of active smallmouth then move to the deep pool. Use your electronics to locate smallmouth and when fish are located use your electric trolling motor to hold you over the fish. Cast a finesse jig or tube slightly upstream and work the bait down into the hole. A red tail chub fished with a few split shots or rigged on a slip sinker is probably the deadliest presentation. I prefer not to anchor since that can spook the larger smallmouth. However, if brisk winds are a problem you might have no other option. When anchoring, make sure that you use ample slack on the line so you can hold the boat over the smallmouth.

Just as with fishing the bridge, pay close attention to the current. If the water is high and you are dealing with a swift current smallmouth can be incredibly shallow. Under lower water conditions and a slower current look for the big smallmouth to be holding on the deep edge of the shoreline rocks or weeds. I avoid fishing deep pools during high water periods since the current makes positioning the boat difficult and, in some cases, impossible.

Fall river smallmouth will cooperate just as well as they do in the summer. The best part, besides their seemingly endless activity, is their size. At no other time of year can anglers expect to catch multiple trophy fish without moving more than a few times. Simply put, if you catch one big smallmouth I guarantee there are more in the area. I personally can't wait for this time of year, even though I know that living in the northwoods my time on the water is limited.

Fishing For Smallmouth Bass

George & Barb 21.5" smallmouth

Ken Kortas   21" smallmouth

Mike Jackson with 2 dandy smallmouth

Charlie Aiello with a midday giant

Fishing For Smallmouth Bass

David Lambrix with a behemoth mid river smallmouth

21" Smallmouth caught by Bob Hayes near a creek channel

Chapter 10
Reservoir Patterns

I touched briefly on fishing reservoirs in the chapter on pre-spawn smallmouth. Reservoirs are also hot beds for smallmouth bass action in summer and fall. While I do fish several reservoirs in summer and fall most of my experience is with natural lakes and rivers. The reservoirs that I fish in the North Country contain stained water as opposed to the clear water reservoirs of the mid-south. One of these years, maybe if I ever retire from guiding I will venture south to investigate one of these southern reservoirs.

One of the most outstanding features in reservoirs regardless of their geographical location is rip rap. Rip rap is usually present around dams, bridges and marinas just to name a few spots. Rip rap can attract smallmouth from ice out to ice up and are worth fishing at anytime. The key to how and when smallmouth will relate to rip rap is forage. This forage can be crayfish or minnows depending on the time of year and individual reservoir.

Most rip rap extends over large areas and can be confusing for a first time angler to fish. If I was on a reservoir for the first time the first place to which I would head would be rip rap and I'd start fishing with a crankbait. When you need to cover water quickly as you search for active fish it is hard to beat a crankbait. Try to match your crankbait with the preferred forage at the time. In my experience, you'd be wise to use both minnow and crayfish imitation crankbaits.

Fishing For Smallmouth Bass

Rip Rap Smallmouth

Once you locate a smallmouth it does not mean that you have found a honey hole. You need to figure out if it was a loner or a school. Stop the boat and continue to cast the crankbait. If after a few casts you come up empty, switch to a tube or grub. If you catch a smallmouth with plastics stay put, but if not, keep on the move and look for another isolated smallmouth and eventually a school.

Find a shoreline point on a reservoir and I can guarantee you will find smallmouth bass. Some points are outstanding features in a reservoir and are easy to spot while others will take a bit of effort. While a noticeable point might attract high numbers of smallmouth they might also receive heavy fishing pressure. An isolated point might not hold as many fish but due to the sparse fishing pressure it can hold larger fish. A variety of presentations will catch smallmouth relating to a point including jigs, drop shot rigs, Carolina rigs and live bait. Other hot prime fishing areas to fish on a reservoir are steep banks, islands, dams and humps.

The shaky head worm technique works well on deep summer smallmouth bass as I once found out on a stained water reservoir. Again, what does a guide do on his day off? He goes fishing! With this time on the water spent in solitude it is the perfect situation to experiment with a new technique. I was surprised, not so much that it worked for smallmouth, but that it caught bass in stained water. Everything I read about fishing the shaky head worm was centered on clear water applications.

On this reservoir there is a rock pile that surges out of 30 feet of water and tops out right at the surface. It is prime area for smallmouth bass and if the conditions are right, an angler using plastics or live bait will find plenty of action. However, in the dog days of summer, which usually means high skies and no wind, good luck. You might find a few smallmouth on the rocks at sunup but for the most part they move out to deep water during the day.

About 50 percent of the time I find these summer smallmouth holding within one foot of the bottom over a sand and rock bottom adjacent to the dam. I had caught several big smallmouth over the years drifting with leeches and with those smallmouth bass that I had caught with the shaky worm fresh in my mind, I was armed and ready. I am always searching for ways to catch smallmouth from this particular reservoir without using live bait in summer.

It was a typical August day with bright sun and no wind. I rigged up a 1/8 ounce shaky head jig with a six inch black finesse worm. I chose a black worm since I knew that smallmouth would inhale a black leech. I positioned the boat over a school of smallmouth and dropped the bait straight down. As soon as the worm hit the bottom I noticed my line moving off to the side and with a sweeping motion set the hook. In a few seconds a huge smallmouth can flying out of the water right in front of the boat. Needless to say I had already made my day after I released a 20 inch smallmouth back into the reservoir. I don't know why, but about 90 percent of the time when I catch a big smallmouth, whether it is in shallow or deep water, it seems as if it is on the first cast that I make in an area. Afterwards, I may catch a few smaller smallmouth, but I seldom catch a hawg.

As I repositioned the boat and dropped the shaky worm back into the stained water, I was certain that when the big smallmouth hit the worm it was sure it was hitting a jumbo leech. On my second cast I could not coax another smallmouth but shortly thereafter I had another pick up and boated an 18 inch smallmouth. I had developed a pattern and I was glad there were no other fishing boats in sight. The only people on the water were pleasure boaters and jet skis, and they had no interest in what I was doing.

My next stop was a steep rock ledge on the deep edge of a point. The top of the point is in five feet of water and the ledge drops to 28 feet. There are several sharp individual ledges on the larger main ledge and I knew from experience that summer smallmouth hold both tight to the bottom and on the granite ledges. I was determined to catch smallmouth on the shaky head jig.

I positioned the boat well out in deep water and made a cast along the granite ledge. I did this several times and did not get any kind of response. I do not have a "side finder" fish locator which will shoot a perpendicular signal from the transducer, enabling the angler to mark fish on ledges. Thus I was unable to establish whether the ledges held any smallmouth or if they were just refusing my presentation.

Although I was unsure of the status of the smallmouth on the ledge, my electronics showed that there was a full house at the base of the ledge. The instant the shaky worm hit the bottom I had a pick up and I set the hook into what would be another 18 inch smallmouth. They were thick on the base of the ledge and I caught four big smallmouth on four consecutive casts. I was starting to like this shaky head worm fishing.

When I was battling my last smallmouth a passing boat stopped. They saw the big smallmouth and the first thing out of one of their mouths was, "What did you catch it on?" They knew who I was and knew that I guided on this reservoir. Since I had already divulged one of my hot spots I did not know what to say. Finally I said, "A shaky head worm." I am sure they were thinking "What on earth is a shaky head worm."

I caught a total of 18 smallmouth on shaky worms that day and all of them were over 17 inches. While I was surprised that I caught that many quality smallmouth what really shocked me was when I hooked a 22 inch walleye. I knew when I hooked the fish it was not a smallmouth but who would ever think that a walleye would hit a shaky worm. I guess that there is a first time for everything. By the way, I did appreciate the walleye that night for dinner. As a matter of fact, this presentation might be worth considering if you are a walleye fisherman.

Shaky head worms do not work well in rivers unless you find smallmouth out of the current. I have experimented with it on a few occasions and while it will catch a smallmouth, there are many other presentations that are more productive.

Reservoirs can hold exceptional smallmouth populations and trophy fish can be common. Don't let the overall size of the reservoir intimidate you. Use a common sense approach and learn a section of the reservoir instead of trying to fish the whole thing in a few days.

Chapter 11
Bridges

One question that is often asked in my seminars is, "Where is the best place to catch a trophy smallmouth?". The best answer I can give to that question is, fish bridges. Bridges have been responsible for many big smallmouth over the years. It does not matter if you are fishing a bridge on a small river or a larger reservoir. If you fish them effectively you will be able to catch big smallmouth. Bridges are an outstanding feature are easy to locate, and are a no brainer for any angler. It amazes me how little fishing pressure bridges receive; even in heavily fished water.

The secret to catching big smallmouth around a bridge is adapting to both the current flow and the season. In spring smallmouth will try to avoid the current as much as possible. Big pre-spawn spring smallmouth will relate to bridges in large numbers. Pre-spawn smallmouth will hold tight to deep cover near a bridge until water temperatures reach 45 degrees. These deep holes are usually associated with rock humps, rubble or wood. The best areas will hold a combination of rock and wood. The more structure, the more smallmouth that will be present but locating them in the cold water will take persistence.

Suitable structure may not be directly under the bridge but upstream or downstream so it might take a bit of searching to locate smallmouth. Use your electronics to locate structure in and adjacent to deep holes. Don't make the mistake of just looking for fish since early pre-spawn smallmouth hold tight to cover. The colder the water and the faster the current the tighter to cover smallmouth will be. Since they are not necessarily feeding you don't need to locate suspended baitfish to find smallmouth. On many occasions I have caught several big smallmouth from deep wood and rubble that my electronics showed held no fish. You will just have to fish an area to find out if anything is present.

Fishing For Smallmouth Bass

The ideal situation is to vertical jig directly over the structure both by drifting and using your electric trolling motor. Keep the presentation as vertical as possible. Walleye anglers are very familiar with this type of presentation but bass anglers often don't get it. This is why walleye fisherman will often catch huge smallmouth, but believe me, it is no accident.

I spend a considerable time in the spring guiding for walleyes and a jig and minnow has resulted in many huge smallmouth. Now when the water is cold and less than desirable weather conditions it is my bait of choice for smallmouth. You will need to experiment with both jig color and size until you find the right combination. If the water is no deeper than 15 feet, I usually stick with round lead head jigs from 1/4 ounce though 3/8 ounce. Top colors are orange, chartreuse, red and white. Tip the jigs with either a fathead or shiner minnow whatever is available. Shiners will catch larger smallmouth but under tough conditions they might prefer a smaller fathead minnow.

If it is impossible to hold over the structure with your trolling motor, anchor up stream, letting out anchor rope to position you over the structure. Another deadly presentation is to position your boat so you can cast upstream and let your bait drift over the cover. This will allow the jig and minnow to drop in the slack water on the downstream side of the cover. If you get light bites on the jig, try a slip sinker rig with a plain Aberdeen hook and a shiner. Remember, big, active smallmouth will hit your presentation on the fall.

Soft plastics can also be deadly for bridge related pre-spawn smallmouth. Tubes are my first choice but fishing them in deep water and current will require extreme patience. Rig the tube either weedless with a wide gap hook and a bullet sinker or a weedless bullet head jig. Once you position your boat over the structure drop the tube into the cover and vertical jig the tube raising it about six to eight inches. The secret is to jig the tube as slowly as possible and get the tube to drop down into the cover. Yes, you will get snagged but that is part of the game. If you use to light a bullet sinker or jighead you will cut down on the snags but the bait won't drop into the strike zone. My favorite tube colors are watermelon red, watermelon, green pumpkin, and any tube with gold or cooper flakes.

Due to the snags I refrain from using braided line since you will be constantly cutting your line. I spool my spinning or casting reel with either fluorocarbon or mono and make sure I have a high quality graphite rod. Fluorocarbon is best due to the increased sensitivity and limited amount of stretch. Once you detect a strike slowly raise the rod and set the hook. If you set the hook to quickly you will miss fish. Mono will work but since you can be dealing with light bites you might miss a few fish and if you are fishing in water deeper than 15 feet line stretch can be a problem. Besides tubes finesse jigs and skirted grubs are also a good choice.

Once the water temperature climbs above 48 degrees smallmouth will move to shallow wood and rock around the bridge. On some days I will start fishing the deeper cover in the morning and by mid day switch to the shoreline cover after the water warms on a bright sunny day. The good thing is that as smallmouth move shallow there activity level rises. Spinnerbaits can be very effective along with stick baits and soft plastic jerkbaits.

Smallmouth continue to relate to bridges after spawning and throughout the summer. The same deep structure that held big smallmouth during the pre-spawn is still productive. Under low water conditions with a limited current deep structure can be dynamite and few anglers give it. Smallmouth will suspend off the bottom allowing the anglers to mark them with their electronics. Just as in the spring use your electric trolling motor or an anchor to position your boat over the fish.

A tube dragged over and around deep bridge cover is a deadly summer tactic. The difference in the summer is that when a smallmouth strikes a tube it is usually an aggressive bite. Even though it is an aggressive bite it is critical not to fish the tube to fast. When you are fishing a tube on the bottom you are resembling a crayfish scrounging lethargically on the bottom. If you are having trouble hooking fish pause a few seconds before setting the hook. As in the spring due to the high number of snags I refrain from using braided line.

For anglers looking to catch a monster smallmouth in summer don't hesitate to try a nightcrawler. On many days the only way to catch these deep smallmouth is with a nightcrawler on a plain hook, with either a slip sinker or a few split shots. Let the nightcrawler drift over the bottom as opposed to letting it sit. The smallmouth are holding in the deep cover, so a nightcrawler sitting effortlessly on the bottom can be counterproductive.

During periods of high water and increased current flow, big smallmouth will hold tight to bridge pilings and shoreline bridge cover just out of the main current and are shy about moving out of the cover to strike a bait. Just as with fishing shoreline cover, the faster the current the tighter the smallmouth will hold to the structure. You will need to cast tight to the structure to connect with smallmouth. If you cast into the current and away from the structure, you will miss contact with the larger smallmouth.

You will need to cast tight or even into the cover with soft plastics so exposed hooks are a no-no. I will use either a stick bait or soft plastic jerkbait rigged with a 4/0 wide gap hook. These salt impregnated baits with their slow horizontal drop will trigger both neutral and active smallmouth. I try to avoid adding any weight to my plastics unless the current is so swift that is will not allow the plastic to fall into the cover. If I need to add weight I will use a weighted wide gap hook. I use both crayfish and minnow imitation colors when choosing stick baits and jerkbaits.

If the current will allow I will wacky rig the stick bait with an off-set bait hook. The wacky worm can be especially deadly in small eddies created by back currents and wing walls around the bridge. When smallmouth are holding in the slack water they will move up in the water column to strike a bait. So be prepared because a smallmouth will hammer the wacky worm as soon as it hits the water.

Submerged wood adjacent to the bridge structure can be a sleeper area for holding a big fish in summer and fall. Just about every bridge you fish will have some type of submerged wood cover. This cover is passed up by most anglers simply because they don't know it exists. It will take patience both to locate this cover and effectively fish it. The bad news is that we are dealing with a river and rivers are constantly changing. I rise in the river and your secret spot is gone. The good news is that high water will bring with a new honey hole and i am constantly watching for new structure to move into my favorite bridges.

You will need to concentrate your efforts on the outer edges of the wood on the edge of the current. Seldom will big smallmouth bury deep into the wood. The same soft plastic jerkbaits and stick baits remain effective but you will need to rig them weedless. I will add a bullet weight to stick bait to allow it to sink down into the cover. You will need to drop the stick bait into the edge of the wood, but if you use too heavy of a weight you will go too deep into the wood cover. Once the stickbait drops into the wood it becomes irrelevant to a smallmouth that is holding on the edge of the wood.

If you are fishing in fast current and smallmouth are tight to structure, spinnerbaits can be very effective. When fishing spinnerbaits, remember that the smallmouth are tight to cover and won't chase very far. Make your cast right on the shoreline. Most of the strikes will occur in the first few turns of the real. One tactic I use is to retrieve the spinnerbait about two feet and then let the bait drop. Many times a big smallmouth will hit the spinnerbait on the drop.

Both blades and the skirt color are important on the spinnerbait. In summer and early fall, smallmouth will be attracted to the spinnerbait both by vibration and sight. In the stained water I fish, chartreuse and white are my favorite colors. Start with a tandem blade spinnerbait, but if you get light strikes go to a single blade spinnerbait.

Over the years some of the most memorable days on the water have occurred while fishing bridges, particularly in the fall. The day I spent with Aaron Mullins tops the list and a feat that I may never top. Aaron was the winner of my fishing contest in 2004, when I had my television show. Being one of many who entered the contest via the internet. The grand prize was a fishing trip and 3 nights stay at a local resort. Besides the trip, Aaron would appear on next year's television show.

I picked up Aaron at the resort and we drove to one of my favorite sections of the river, where we met my camera man, Brian Whitens. Now, Aaron lives in my area, so he was familiar with this stretch of the river. He assured me that he would keep where we were fishing confidential. I knew we had excellent conditions but did not know how good they would be.

There was a nip of frost in the air and the river level had risen a bit overnight. After a short boat ride, we came to a bridge; that I explained to Aaron that it had been holding lots of smallmouth. We rigged up red tail chubs, and quickly began catching big smallmouth. I think Aaron made four casts and caught four big smallmouth. I got into the act and also began catching fish after fish. In 40 minutes we caught and released 30 smallmouth with half of them measuring over 18 inches. We had several doubles and if there would have been a third angler in the boat we would have had triples. I am sure Brian would have like to put down the camera and get into the action.

Now, I had fished the bridge a few days earlier and we caught several nice smallmouth, but they were holding tight to the bottom. If our presentation was not right on the bottom, we did not catch a fish. Today, with the increased current, smallmouth were holding tight to the concrete wall. The rising water had pushed baitfish tight to the wall, and the smallmouth were on the feed. This is a typical fall scenario on a bridge.

Bridges have also been responsible for the largest fish of the day on many occasions. Even on days when the action was consistent throughout the day, the bridge was still the place to be, like one day I fished with John Fincato and his wife Jo from Ohio.

Fishing For Smallmouth Bass

We were having a great day catching nice smallmouth almost everywhere we fished. Just about all the smallmouth we caught were running big, and they had been some of the largest fish John had ever encountered. What made the day interesting was that every time we went back to the bridge we caught a smallmouth at least 20 inches. Each big smallmouth we caught, was exactly in the same spot. They were holding just out of the current over submerged wood.

Smallmouth will also relate to both wood and weeds upstream and downstream from the bridge. Weeds in particular can hold large numbers of smallmouth. You don't need to search for large weed beds since even small patches can attract both baitfish and crayfish. Smallmouth will scatter in these weeds so you will need to work the entire area and keep on the move. This is an excellent place to work a surface bait. If you have a good weed edge and mix it with some downed wood you may have a real winner.

Also keep your eyes on both the shoreline and locator, looking for the remains of previous bridges. Old bridges are replaced and their remains can be just upstream or downstream from the new bridge. Isolated rock and rubble can be a magnet for smallmouth and other anglers may just pass it by. The older the rubble, the more logs and debris, that will be mixed in. I have been fishing areas like this on my home river for years, and even many of my clients do not realize why the fish are there.

If you learn anything I hope you never pass up a bridge again. While the bridge may hold smallmouth spring through fall you will need to refine your approach. Again, never hit the water without making a few trips to your favorite bridge. The only problem is that bridges can be high traffic areas and tend to get a fair amount of fishing pressure.

Chapter 12
Guide Tales

To this day, I do not know why I chose this occupation except for the fact that I could not hold a job because I spent too much time on the water. I figured that as long as I was going to fish every day, I might as well try to make a living at it. I have been guiding for 30 years, have chalked up a great deal of experience, and can deal with almost any situation but I still haven't figured out which is the greater challenge; trying to catch fish or accommodating the public. All kidding aside, I love my job and wouldn't do anything else; however, there are times when I wish I would have had a real job.

Guiding is not for everyone and for the most part it attracts all types of individuals to our chosen occupation. Many a fishing guide has left a well-paying real job or profitable business to deal with less than grateful clients who think you have the ability to perform miracles. Some people even go so far as to accuse you of being a crook when they pay you for a day when the fish don't bite. There are no two fishing guides alike, and each one has their own unique perspective on how to both catch fish and deal with the public. To better understand this book you have to understand certain tricks of the trade. It took me years to figure out this stuff.

Keep in mind that most clients think that once you acquire a guide's license you miraculously know everything there is about catching fish. Since they are in the boat with a professional guide, they reason that there should never be anything close to a slow day on the water. All the guide has to do is wave their magic wand, which comes with the purchase of a guide license, and the fish respond to their needs. Once you have every fish in the lake under your command, all the client has to do is place an order as to how many and how big the fish will be. I kid you not, there are some people who really believe that when they hire a fishing guide all they need to do is show up and they will limit out and get a fish for the wall with little, if any, effort on their part.

The first thing on the agenda is booking the guide. Ninety percent of people who hire a guide are very serious about their trip and communicating as much as possible with the guide prior to the trip is good for both the guide and the client. A guide will help his client prepare for the trip and suggest to the client the proper lures and tackle to bring along for a successful outing. Most clients also know that they are going fishing and that fishing is not an exact science but, they like to be prepared. Most anglers also like to buy a few new baits before a trip which helps keep the tackle shops in business.

Some people call or e-mail to inquire about rates, availability, etc. and book a trip but then don't communicate with their guide until a week or so before the trip. Other people are in constant contact with the guide. It is not the number of times that the client contacts the guide but the nature of the questions that becomes more than telling to an experienced guide. There are a few red flags that pop up that can almost guarantee a tough day on the water for the guide. How a guide handles his clients prior to the outing is critically important to a pleasant experience for guide and client alike.

If your client mentions more than one bad fishing experience during those initial communications, the experienced guide will know he might have a problem. This lets the guide know that the potential client is one of those people who is never happy. These types of people seem to experience a bad trip no matter where they go. Over the years I have come to the conclusion that some people are impossible to please. These same people that are a nightmare for a fishing guide are usually a pain in the rear for a waitress, bartender, shop keeper or resort owner. The problem is that a fishing guide has to give the client their immediate attention for the entire day, while the other people can move on to other costumers. A boat can sometimes become a very small space by the end of the day.

The client won't really ask a question, just tell you about how the fishing was less than desirable or that the guide persisted in doing things his way. They are looking for a place to fish that is loaded with fish and, regardless of the time of year and prevailing weather, they want to fish *their* way. What this communicates immediately is that this guy thinks that he knows more than the guide he hired on his last trip and he probably knows more about my home water than I do. The fact that I have been fishing these waters for over 30 years will never enter his mind, his ego is already his own worst enemy.

Sometimes it is hard to distinguish between a sensible question and one that can cause a problem down the road. For example, if the client asks you how many smallmouth are caught on a typical average day make sure you have a lot of leeway in the answer. If you give him a definite answer he may hold you to your word. One time I told a guy we would catch about 25 Smallmouth and he caught 20. When we concluded the day he kept commenting about how slow the day was as if he wanted me to knock off a few bucks. I finally shut him up when I started talking about the ten or twenty fish that he missed due to his incompetence. I ticked him off, but it did not bother me since I knew he would not be a repeat customer. Now when people call I tell them we should catch between 15-30 smallmouth on an average day.

I have even had people ask me how many muskies they will catch in a day. Now that is definitely a red flag. This guy has been watching way too many television shows and does not live in the real world. So now when a potential client asks me that question I respond by saying, "That depends on how big you want them to be."

Another red flag that signals trouble is when the potential client lets you know of all the big fish that he has caught over the years. This is the guy who has been everywhere and has caught bigger fish than the guides he fished with. The client spends more time bragging about himself than he does asking questions about his potential trip. He lets you know that he only catches big fish but he is bringing along a friend who is less experienced and his friend will be happy to catch anything. I've learned that most people who act like this are probably feeling some anxiety about fishing with a professional guide, but rather than simply being honest with themselves and the guide about their true ability they try to cover up their inability by bragging or by deflecting attention away from themselves and onto their "inexperienced" partner.

However, not to throw a wrench into my theory, but I have had people who made me go into panic mode when they first called me but then they turned out to be great customers. On the other hand, I have had people call who led me to believe that we were going to have a great day on the water, and yet the day turned out to be a nightmare. Some of the clients I thought would be a nightmare have turned out to be regular clients who have fished with me for years.

You also have to watch your blind side for the guy who is pumping you for information but has no intention of ever using your services. This is actually a common occurrence, especially now with the internet. These guys are quite creative and they can be convincing as they talk about possible bookings and pry you for fishing information at the same time. Sometimes I think these guys figure if they call enough guides they will find one or two that will be naive enough to give them the information they desire. In my younger days I was eager to book anyone and I would spill the beans about places I fish, and what secret tactics I use to catch fish. Actually, for an experienced guide these people are easy to pick up on and if the guide is smart he can play along with the guy and give him as much bogus information as possible. In this stage of my career I enjoy the challenge and can find the humor in some of ridiculous games people try to play with me.

One winter I had a guy call several times about booking me for smallmouth fishing on the Menominee River. I can't remember the guy's name but looking back on it now, it probably was a false identity. He did e-mail me a few times but he probably figured that he could get more information through phone conversations. Each time he called he was insistent about how he was going to book me several times throughout the year to get a handle on the smallmouth patterns during the spring, summer and fall. After the second call, I figured out his motive, and since he was paying for the call, I figured that it was time to have some fun.

At the start of the call he would start the conversation asking about which days I had open during a specific month. Next, he would start asking about what part of the river *we* would fish during that time, and what boat landing I would use for access. Next he went into the type of lures, colors and other related topics. I am sure he was jotting things down as we talked and after about five phone conversations he figured he had the river down pat. After the fifth phone call I never heard from him again.

While he might have thought he put one over on me, I had the last laugh. When he asked about spring fishing spots I told him to fish places I fish in late summer. For summer spots I divulged a few places where he would catch carp and suckers. For fall trophy spots I sent him to spring spots. Best of all I told him to buy all kinds of lures that I never caught any fish on no matter how often I tried. I specified lures that were expensive with outrageous color patterns that would never work on the river. Obviously, our paths never crossed since we were on opposite ends of the river. I only wish Bass Pro Shops knew how many sales they ran through due to me; they could have at least sent me a gift certificate for a sales commission.

Another winter I had had a walleye fishermen call me several times inquiring about a spring walleye trip on the Menominee River. Again, each time he called he started asking if I still had the dates open that he tentatively told me to pencil in saying that he would send a deposit shortly.

Suddenly the conversation moved to which area of the river would be best. I explained that it all depended on the conditions and that there was not one magic spring spot. He would ask me where we would fish high water conditions, low water conditions, medium water conditions and after a cold front. Finally I told him that we would continue our conversation at a later date after I received his deposit to hold the penciled in date. Guess what! I never heard for him again.

All anglers learn very quickly that the weather has an effect on fishing. They go out on a lake, they have a slow day and they blame it on a cold front. I have used the weather for an excuse for more days of bad fishing than I would like to admit. Sure there are many days when inclement weather conditions can put a damper on fishing regardless of the anglers' ability. However, for a guide the number one factor in the amount of fish put in the boat is the ability of the client.

Once you actually get into the boat and start fishing, a guide has to rate his client's ability. Forget about all the prior phone conversations and e-mails where the client let the guide know about their expertise because the proof will be in the pudding. The quicker the guide gets a handle on the client's ability, the quicker the clients can start catching fish. This is one significant advantage that the regular client has. If the guide is familiar with the client he can put them on fish once the boat hits the water. The greater the comfort zone is between the guide and the client, the better it is for both of them.

The trick is for the guide to rate the client's ability without the guide letting the client know what he is doing. Rule number one: the guide has to be careful not to insult his client regardless of their ability. A good guide will be able to adapt to people with all kinds of fishing abilities. A guide has to work with the cards they were dealt. It can be a challenge and test all your patience, but as I had one client tell me, "That is why I am paying you."

The guide needs to understand the individual needs of his clients. I break my clients down into three categories, the seasoned angler, average and the novice. All three categories are distinctly different and need to be approached with a different perspective. When you are dealing with two or three people in the boat you will be dealing with different client ratings and you will need to tend to each client's needs.

For the most part the seasoned angler is the easiest to deal with. They are people who have fished extensively with guides over the years and understand how things work. They know that the weather effects fish and that even under the most ideal conditions there are still some days the fish just don't bite. Seasoned anglers know that if they keep focused on fishing that eventually things can start to happen and a slow day can turn into a great day very quickly. Most anglers think they fit into this category but unfortunately only about 25 percent of the people I deal with fall into this category. If 100 percent of my clients fell into this category my job would be all the easier since they usually land their own fish and tie on all their own tackle.

Most of the people I deal with fall into the average category. This means they do a fair amount of fishing and have some sort of understanding of how things work. They know that the fish do not always bite and you have to stick it out in order to catch fish. Much of the success rate for the day will depend on their casting ability and their feel for the days' bite. A guide can work with them on an individual basis to help them get a feel for things, but for the most part the ball is in their court. One person can catch on quickly while another struggles and it can make for a frustrating day. This can be a good or bad day on the water, with most of it being out of your control.

We are left finally to deal with those clients who fall into the category of being a novice. Like the seasoned angler, this category of fishermen compiles about 25 percent of my business. Actually, I enjoy these guide trips as long as the people are eager to learn. I believe that most guides are like me in this regard in that they get more satisfaction out of watching other people catch fish than catching fish themselves. On most of these guide trips if you can catch people a few nice fish and supply some sort of action, they are usually happy; at least most of the time.

Problems arise when the novice client has set their expectations too high and you are thus hit with a tough fishing day. I understand that they figure they are hiring a pro and he has the solution to all the problems that can arise, thinking that the guide can work miracles. Maybe they have been watching too many television shows where the featured anglers catch a ton of fish in a half hour show. All a guide can do is give it everything they have and hope for the best.

On more than a few occasions you will need to deal with a client with average ability at best but who thinks that he is ready to turn pro. Much of the success rate of a guide's client depends on the client's willingness to listen to the guide. Most people are on the water to have a good time and are eager to learn. However, after 30 years of guiding I still get the occasional client who prefers to use his favorite baits and does not respond to my suggestions. I have never figured out why people like this hire a guide.

Of course, at the end of the day, their poor catch rate is the guides' fault and had nothing to do with them being pigheaded.

A case in point was one August day on the Menominee River. Following a few days of stable weather a small summer cold front passed through and I knew that the topwater bite would slow down. To make matters worse, my clients for the next few days were contrarians and had their own way to catch smallmouth. We started out fishing with wacky rigged four-inch Case Magic Sticks and tubes. The bite was slow early in the day but improved as the morning progressed. I could see my clients were getting anxious to fish topwater, since they both said they did not like to fish plastics.

I told them that one of them should tie on a topwater bait. Now, these guys had fished with me before, and I knew that the one guy in particular had no patience for pause and stop retrieve. His idea of fishing topwater was to bulge his buzz bait as fast as possible making about six casts to my one. While they insisted that I did not fish, I made a few casts with a Hubs Chub to show them the proper retrieve. On the second cast I connected with a nice 18 inch smallmouth and I retired my rod.

Most of my clients would have asked for one of the baits on which I had just caught the smallmouth, but not this guy. A buzzbait went flying over my head, landed in a downed tree and the buzz bait was doing its thing, not catching any smallmouth. Finally, I convinced him to tie on a Hubs Chub and he caught a few smallmouth. However, he said he did not like to fish this way, went back to the buzz bait and caught no fish. Here is a case where if my clients would have left their tackle boxes at home and used my baits of choice we would have put more fish in the boat.

Regardless of the client's ability a guide has to treat each client as a potential repeat customer. So the quicker you figure out the needs of the client the greater the odds of the survival of your livelihood.

Once you have established the client's ability, next you have to feel him out as to how trustworthy he is. This will require another classification since a guide has to protect the water that he is fishing. If you take a guy to a spot that holds lots of fish, it might not hold lots of fish in the future if the client returns to the spot and cleans out the honey hole. So the guide has to use a bit of restraint if he intends to stay in business. That is why I rate my spots Class A, B and C.

Class "A' spots are those places that are definitely not for every client. This is the spot that can make or break a guide trip, but unfortunately they are the most vulnerable spots. That is why many a first time customer never sees a class "A" spot. The only first time clients that see a class "A" spot is someone who travels a long distance and is not likely to return in the immediate future. If the customer does not own a boat he is also a safe bet. Most guides also have a few class "AA" spots that they have to protect with your life for that day when you need a big fish and fast. The less often a guide fishes these spots the better they are.

Class "B" spots are the most common and are the staple for most fishing spots. These spots will regularly produce steady action and they have the potential to produce a trophy fish. While these spots are numerous a guide still has to be careful as to the amount of pressure he puts on the spot. If you fish the spot too many consecutive days in a row, even if the fish are released, the fish eventually need a rest. I feel that you can work a good spot for two days before it needs a rest.

A class "C" spot is a spot that usually holds fish but they are nothing to get excited about. These are the spots that I usually start fishing so I can get the feel of the client. If I feel that the client will return to the spot and keep smallmouth, the client will probably spend the day fishing class "C" spots. Once I establish that I am fishing with a safe client I can move on to a class "B" spot. If throughout the day I get the feel that the client is going to return, I might consider moving into a class "A" spot to catch the fish of the day. If in your own guiding you don't take the client to the class "A" spot you can at least mention that you have this big fish spot in another part of the river in hopes of sealing the deal for the next guide trip.

Then there is the cooler fisherman. This is the guy that wants to catch a boat load of fish and load up the cooler. While they enjoy the outdoors, they rate their day by the amount of fish in the cooler at the end of the day. In the past I have had people actually comment about the fact that they have a big cooler to fill. These people are dangerous enough while walleye fishing, but I try to avoid them altogether while smallmouth fishing. The cooler fisherman is usually a one-time client so if you don't catch lots of fish to fill up the cooler it is no big deal. I would rather have a slow day on the water than let a client go home with a cooler full of smallmouth.

A good guide has many methods of protecting his livelihood from clients who either refuse to listen to the advice of the guide, or, who given the opportunity, would fillet every fish they could catch. Some people think they are sharp and watch every move that I make trying to figure out my game plan. While this is a smart thing to do, they do not understand that I catch on to them quickly and always have a few tricks up my sleeve to make things look far more complicated than they really are. It is often a challenge to try to confuse somebody who is trying to figure out what I am doing. It took me years to master these tricks and since each client is different I never feel that my job is boring.

Anyone who has ever wet a line is always searching for that secret spot. You know, the place that is loaded with fish and nobody else knows about it. Well, I must confess, I have stumbled upon a few of these over the years and somehow managed not to keep them a secret. After all, I am in business to make a buck and somehow my interest in making money caused me to search for these hidden waters in hopes of making happy clients. If I was rich, I suppose I could have kept these secret lakes to myself, but then I would have had no need to find them in the first place.

For years I have had clients who assume each year that I will take them to new water. Each year I would hear the same comments from the same guys: "When are you going to take me to the good spot?" While I live in an area that abounds in water, good fishing holes are not all that easy to find. Sometimes I think that my clients think that I can pull a secret lake out of a hat. There is a fine line that can make a fishing hole go from good to great. Many times it is just a matter of catching a big fish, or should I say that the client actually catches the fish instead of screwing up and letting the fish get away. It's one of those things that are out of the guide's control.

So, what does a guide do on his day off? Go fishing of course! Besides getting some peace of mind it allows me to search out new water. I might fish a stretch of river that I have never fished before, a stretch that I have not fished in a few years, or a quote "wilderness lake". City people love to hear the word wilderness. To them a wilderness lake is one surrounded by trees and only a few cabins. When I take them to a wilderness lake, and they catch fish, it is a winner for both of us even if the lake is just a few miles from a County Highway. Mix in a deer, porcupine and the call of a loon and they are really awed.

If your clients are real city dudes then you can really have some fun. I have been known to add a few miles of gravel roads onto my drive to add a bit of wilderness effect. By the time we get to the landing they are all wound up and raring to go. This extended drive has a dual purpose. First off, it does add to the adventure, but more importantly, it can confuse a client and make it harder for him to return to the honey hole on his own. The worse the road is the better. And of course, everyone always asks, "How did you find this place." The trick is to let them think that they were the first people that I ever took to that spot.

Most of the time things go as planned, but on occasion I have to talk my way out of it, like the time I launched the boat at a primitive boat landing on a Menominee River backwater. It was early May and the trees were barren since they had not yet sprouted their summer foliage. Visibility was great and you could see in the woods for over a mile. We were fishing a shoreline for smallmouth when my client heard a logging truck roaring across a paved highway. As he gazed at the truck he asked me if that was a boat landing over in the bay. I quickly replied, "Yes, that is a landing but it is much too shallow to launch my boat." I quickly veered the boat to the right in order to block his view of the boat landing. I did not want him to see the paved landing and newly constructed courtesy pier. He just looked at me and chuckled, made a cast and caught an 18 inch smallmouth.

The problem with taking a client to a secret lake is that they expect the guide to perform miracles. After all, you are taking them to a place loaded with fish that you searched out just to satisfy their need to catch large numbers of trophy fish. They assume that no other anglers will be on the water and the fish will jump in the boat regardless of their fishing ability or the weather conditions. My clients will also assume that the secret lake that I take them to is just for them and not my other clients. One guy went so far as to suggest that I never take any other anglers to this spot except for him. He assumed that if I overfished the spot he would not be able to bring his buddies to the spot. So when you tell your client that you are taking them to a secret lake your reputation is often on the line.

I have been burned many times over the years by clients who have no interest in using my services more than once. They feel they will pay the money, learn the hot spot and go and tell all their buddies. These are usually people who have a cabin in the area or have fished my local waters before. It is a smart move, since what they can learn in a day on the water with a local guide could take years of fishing on their own. Besides learning new fishing spots, the guide will show them hot baits and special techniques that apply to a specific body of water. Experience has taught me over the years that only good clients go to those secret lakes. Sometimes you learn the hard way.

When talking about secret lakes, no place fits the bill better than one small reservoir hidden in the Northwoods well off the beaten path. I had fished the reservoir through the years and it used to have a phenomenal walleye population. It was one of those places where I could take a reliable client or friend and they were guaranteed to catch walleyes regardless of what Mother Nature threw our way. I knew that once the word was out, it would not take long to fish the reservoir out, primarily due to its small size. Unfortunately, I blame myself for leading to this particular reservoirs' demise. Yes, a guide has to do what he has to, but taking the wrong client to a hotspot will come home to haunt you big time!

One day I ran into a guy in a tavern and we started to talk about the fishing on one of my home lakes-- High Falls Flowage. The guy told me that he had fished High Falls for 20 years and now lamented that his favorite spots no longer yielded him a limit of walleyes. He was from the Green Bay area and the fact that he had a cabin not far from the flowage enabled him to fish it on a regular basis. I had seen him on the water many times but had never talked with him. After he bought me several beers he began prying me for information about the other waters that I fished. Usually, I can talk my way around these situations but this guy was good and I eventually put my foot in my mouth.

We started to talk about fishing on the Menominee River and I told him that the spring walleye fishing on the river was much better than on High Falls. Now, please understand that this guy was pretty slick and very persistent and that, along with countless beers he also bought me lunch. He knew I had a few secret places that were my ace in a hole and this guy had an agenda. Bear in mind that this was winter and the checking account was getting pretty low. He said that he would give me a hundred dollar deposit right then if I promised that I would take him to one of my secret lakes. Being that I only had twenty bucks in my pocket, it was an offer I could not refuse. After another beer, I put the hundred dollar bill in my pocket and headed for home. Any day I can put a hundred dollar bill in my pocket during the winter is a good day for me.

He called me a few days later and we set up a date. We talked for a while and everything seemed in order until I started to think about it. The fact that he was concerned about taking home a limit of walleyes should have been a red flag. Basically, these Cooler Fishermen judge success by the number of fish in the cooler. They fill the cooler full of beer before heading out on the water, empty the cooler during the days' fishing and fill the cooler full of fish at the end of the day. Bonding with nature or the challenge of figuring out the days' fishing pattern is not on their agenda. It also concerned me that all of the clients that I had taken to this spot were from out of town and did not own boats of their own. Booking George would turn out to be one of the worst mistakes I had ever made with a client.

The reservoir is small, covering only 180 acres, and it has only one major inlet. The inlet is a trout stream which usually has high water in the spring. Walleyes will travel about four miles to spawn below a water fall. While there are a few rock and gravel areas throughout the reservoir none of it seems to be suitable for walleye spawning. I estimate that well over 90 percent of the walleyes in the reservoir would spawn below the waterfall. Sometimes the fishing can be too good!

George booked a mid-week date and I knew we would have the reservoir to ourselves. After I launched the boat we headed to a narrow inlet on the west end of the reservoir. I slowed the boat down and told George that we would have to navigate upstream with caution for a few miles. I used the old guide trick of telling my client that the navigation in the river was actually much worse than it was. This often will deter a client from returning with his own boat. So after zigzagging in the river and avoiding a few boulders we finally arrived at a waterfall.

I tossed out the anchor and told George to make a cast towards the current break a few feet from the shoreline. He made a perfect cast and connected with a fish. It was a 23 inch female walleye that still had eggs. He wanted to keep the walleye but I assured him that we would catch plenty of smaller male walleyes that would be great for the pan. Before I could say anything George had the fish in the livewell. About that time I shook my head and I knew that I was in trouble, or should I say that the reservoir was in trouble.

It did not take long for George to have five walleyes in my livewell and I also had a few. He caught another walleye and proceeded to place it in the livewell. I told him that he already had is limit and he said "So what!"

George replied, "This is a weekday and there won't be any wardens around."

I responded, "Release that walleye." I assured him that he could continue to fish, but insisted quite emphatically that he could not put any more walleyes in the livewell. I was beginning not to like this guy.

We caught a ton of walleyes the rest of the day but there was very little conversation between us. The ride home was tough because he knew, that I knew, that he would return. When we got back to his vehicle at a local restaurant where we had met earlier in the day, George paid me and went on his way. I knew I would see him again, but hopefully not on the water.

A week later I took another reliable client to the reservoir. We navigated upstream to the falls and began catching and releasing several nice walleyes and even put a few eaters in the livewell. Suddenly I heard a humming noise and told my client that it sounded like an outboard. Well, I was wrong; it was three boats full of fisherman! You guessed it, my old client George was leading the flotilla.

I told my client that whatever these guys did, that we were holding tight to this spot. Sure enough, George got as close to me as possible and started making casts within inches of ours. Before I could say anything his buddies were also crowding in on us. I knew that they were not just trying to catch the fish under my boat, but were trying to push me out of my spot. If they made me miserable they figured I would leave.

They neglected the fact that I had no place to go. This was the spot, and I was not going to leave. It did not take long and I could hear the beer cans popping one after another, and the stooges started to become obnoxious. George did not say much and tried to avoid eye contact with me throughout the day. However, nothing can put a damper on a days' fishing quicker than being thirty yards away from a couple of boatloads of drunks. It was amazing, but we were all catching fish and, as annoyed as I was, since the action continued I was able to keep my cool. I thought about moving just to get away from the crowd, but I would be giving way to a bunch of ignoramuses.

Although we had caught lots of walleyes, it was not an enjoyable day on the water. On the ride home I apologized to my client and told him that one of the guys had fished with me previously. My client said it was not my fault that they were such pinheads and that the situation was out of my control. We did figure out that there were eight guys in those boats which would make their legal limit 40 walleyes between them. We both agreed that they probably were all well over their limit. In fact, one of the boats left for a while and returned. We figured that they had made a run back to the landing to unload some walleyes.

I told my client that I anticipated a run back to the boat landing by at least one of the boats. This anticipated run was the main reason I kept my cool. I told my client that it would not have taken much to push one of these guys over the edge and that there was no telling what they could have done to my truck back at the landing.

Yes, unfortunately, it was like catching fish in a barrel and I knew that showing George this spot would lead to trouble. I guess every now and then a guide gets bamboozled and you just have to chalk it up to experience. I fished that spot for a few years after that and watched it quickly go downhill. I bet George is still trying to find someone on whom to blame the poor fishing. Who knows? He may even blame me for all I know rather than accept any responsibility for over-fishing the spot.

To this day I have a few spots on the river that I save only for a reliable client or a friend that I can trust. Although you can never fish out an entire river, you can destroy a particular spot for years on end. These secret places on the river are special and I have to protect them with my life. I may even have a spot or two that I am afraid to take anyone. However, when the fishing is slow and you have a paying client you have to do the right thing. It's pretty tough to avoid a spot you know is loaded with fish. The trick is to let the client think that you just stumbled onto the fish as you tell him that this is the first time you ever caught fish in that particular spot. Sometimes it works to your advantage to play stupid.

Talking about playing stupid, I have been conned a few times over the years by clients. You know, the guy that pretends that he has never fished on the river before and has no intentions of doing so in the future. He just decided to give me a call so he and his buddy could catch a few fish. While in the boat they try to become my lifelong friend and once they depart forget that they ever knew me. The guy who tries to conceal his GPS in his pocket and doesn't think I notice him fumbling around each time we fish a new spot. I can usually put a stop to that without saying a word. A few intimidating stares will keep the GPS in the pocket. Sometimes actions are better than words.

Getting burned by a guy like George is one thing but having your trust betrayed by a friend is another story. I grew up in the old school that when you considered a guy a friend that you developed a trust in each other, especially when you are dealing with the way one of you makes a living. Again, I guess I have had to learn the hard way. Nothing fits the bill to illustrate my point quite like the story of the three brothers from Chicago.

At a sports show in Chicago I ran into an old friend of mine that I had not seen for about 15 years. Al and I had fished together years back when I lived in the Chicago area and, for the most part, I had good memories. After a long chat with Al and his friend Mark, they booked a couple of days in early October when I assured them that I had a hotspot that held a load of big smallmouth and walleyes.

When October arrived the party had grown from two to four people. Al and Mark would fish with me in my boat and Mark's two brothers would fish out of their boat. Everything seemed fine since a follow boat is nothing out of the ordinary. I was slightly ticked since they waited until that morning to tell me about the extra boat, but since Al was a friend, I did not take issue with it.

We had a good ride to the landing and Al and Mark drove with me. On the way to the river Mark kept stressing the fact that he and his brothers were total catch and release fisherman. I told them that if we caught some

171

eating sized walleye they could feel free to keep them. Mark said that that would not happen since neither he nor his brothers ate fish. Now, being that Al was a friend and Mark said that he and his brothers did not ever keep any fish, you would think I was safe in taking them to one of my good spots. I must admit though that that was the first time I ever took four guys fishing and three of them said they never ate fish. One guy yes, but three guys going fishing and none of them being fish eaters should have been a red flag. I'm either way too trusting, a slow learner or both.

The first day was an excellent day on the water. The first spot we fished was a steep shoreline on the edge of a large slough off the Menominee River. I explained to Al and Mark that we would use my electric trolling motor to hold us within casting distance of the shoreline and cast our red tail chubs tight to the wood. The other boat with Mark's brother positioned about 40 yards upstream would adopt the same presentation.

It did not take long for us to start catching some behemoth smallmouth. The action was hot and heavy and our boat caught over 40 smallmouth in the 17-20 inch class. Just when you'd think that it could not get any better, Mark hooked into a 31 inch walleye. We took plenty of pictures and Mark asked me if he could keep the walleye for mounting. I agreed to letting Mark keep the fish in spite of the fact that walleyes that big are rare on the river. It was a big female that was well past her reproductive years.

Mark's brothers pulled alongside our boat to admire the big walleye and they hoisted up a 22 inch smallmouth and a 27 inch walleye which they released. Besides the walleyes they said that they had caught 25 good sized smallmouth. We all had caught enough fish for the day and headed back to the boat landing. Everyone was in a great mood on the ride home and we talked about our plan to return to the spot the next day.

We hit the water around the same time the following day and, needless to say, our excellent luck continued. Throughout the day I pointed out the marks on the mouths of a few of the smallmouth noting that they had been caught yesterday. Even though I was under the assumption that these guys practiced catch and release, I felt it was a point of interest. While we did not catch any walleyes the second day, one of Mark's brothers tied into a 40 inch northern pike. So in the two days we boated a 10 pound walleye, a few six pound smallmouth and a 20 pound northern pike. This is great fishing in anyone's book.

I fished that stretch of river with a client a few days the following week and again had great fishing. Everything looked in order until the following Friday when I pulled into the boat landing and saw Mark's brother's truck and boat trailer parked next to the ramp. At first I did not panic since I assumed that they would be releasing their fish, although I was a little bit annoyed since I knew they would be in my spot.

As I rounded the bend and saw the red Lund camped out on that steep shoreline adjacent to the slough I admit that I was slightly ticked. As I passed the boat, Mark and his brothers crunched over with their back towards me as if I was not going to recognize them. I didn't expect them to wave at me and toot their horn, but how stupid do they think I am? I guess I should have stopped and asked them if the fish were biting or if they knew of any good spots on the river to fish.

I headed for the next slough, which encompassed a small creek mouth. I was a good spot and one that I did not show Mark and his brothers so I felt confident it would hold some nice smallmouth. It wasn't where I wanted to start, but a spot I probably would have fished later in the day. Nevertheless, my client started to catch fish after a few casts, though I must admit that I could not get that other spot were the red Lund was fishing off my mind.

After about an hour, I noticed a lot of commotion in the red Lund off in the distance. Being nosey, I picked up my binoculars and to my amazement watched Mark flip a big smallmouth into the livewell. Now they had my attention. I continued to watch them for the next hour or so as they loaded up the livewell. By noon they were gone, probably with a limit of 15 smallmouth.

On Saturday I decided to fish another stretch of river since I was almost certain that Mark and his brothers would be camped out on that spot. Granted, they had not broken any laws but they would interfere with my fishing and ruin my day. The stretch of river that we fished on Saturday was a good one and we caught plenty of big smallmouth.

On Monday I returned to that steep shoreline on the edge of the slough and while we did catch some smallmouth they tended to run smaller. We did catch a few 20 inch smallmouth and all in all while it was a good day, it wasn't a fantastic one. In my mind I figured that Mark and his brothers had caught somewhere in the neighborhood of 30 to 50 smallmouth. I am sure that they went home with a cooler full of trophy sized smallmouth fillets.

I fished the stretch of river several times that fall and spent considerable time on that part of the river the following year. It seemed like the fishing went down on each trip. By the way, I did see that red Lund on the river every Friday, Saturday or Sunday that I fished that stretch. I did some research and found out that they were saying at a local motel just about every weekend in September and October. Finally, I admitted defeat and abandoned the spot.

I don't think Al ever returned to that spot but his friend Mark and his brothers returned many times. In fact, from what I could see they were fishing the spot every weekend. Each time I launched my boat and saw the red suburban and the Shorelander trailer I knew there would be a few less fish in the spot. Here again, four guys taking home a limit does not sound bad until you figure that they had done this 10 to 12 times in a year likely resulting in 40 to 50, 18 to 21 inch smallmouth going under the fillet knife; and who knows how many walleye and pike were added into the total fish kill?

I continued to see them fishing that stretch of the river for a few years after that but I surrendered the river to them since my catch rate became so low. The only good thing was that they were not very good fisherman and could not connect the dots. They were not wise enough to search out new stretches of river and look for similar areas to fish. Thank God that I did not take them to any other spots. It's pretty bad when people have to lie to the guide by telling him that they don't eat fish in hopes that he will take them to his secret spot.

Many of these secret lakes and secret spots on the river are hidden and hard to find. Even if a client does return to a spot on his own he will have trouble zeroing in on the fish. A smart guide will not say anymore than he has to. You might take a client to a spot after a cold front and catch a ton of fish, but you don't have to tell him that the spot is only good after a September cold front when the river level rose a few inches overnight and the maples are starting to turn. Take one of these variables out of the equation and the fish will be down-river hiding behind a stump. If the maple trees have lost their leaves big smallmouth will stack up under an overhanging oak tree. These are the things that take years of on the water experience to learn and enable me to catch lots of big fish each year. I only wish it was that easy!

Sometimes a hot spot is no secret and is impossible to camouflage no matter what you do. Even if I drive a few extra miles, talk about the recent bear attacks, or how the spot is a magnet for tornados, the spot is so good odds are that some clients will return. Some spots are like catching fish out of a barrel, regardless of your ability, and are far too convenient for a client to return even if they do not own a boat. Unfortunately, it is one of those places to which I have my regrets for taking people over the years, like the time I shot myself in the foot when I took Oscar and the guys from Arkansas to the spot.

Oscar had looked at my website several times before he gave me a call. Through our phone conversation I got the impression that Oscar was an avid smallmouth bass fisherman and that he was impressed by the gargantuan size of the smallmouth that I catch in the river. He told me that back in Arkansas a 17 inch smallmouth was considered big and I assured him that that is just an average sized smallmouth on the river. I just take for granted that anyone concerned about quality smallmouth bass is into catch and release. Not that Oscar and his buddies weren't good guys it is just that that they were cooler fishermen.

I met the guys at a mini mart since it is an easy location to find as well as being a good place to pick up a few snacks and beverages. As I pulled up they were dumping a bag of ice into a large cooler. I nicely hinted that the cooler was a bit large to bring into the boat. Oscar replied, "This is for the fish." While they might not have had a cooler full of beer, which I do not allow in my boat, it was obvious they were anticipating smallmouth bass fillets for supper.

My clients loaded their fishing gear into my boat, Oscar jumped in the truck with me and his buddy followed me in their truck with the cooler full of ice. On the way to the landing I had to make a quick decision as to where I was going to take these guys. Oscar mentioned a couple of times that he would be a return customer and he had many friends back in Arkansas that inquired about my services. While I had heard this many times before, being that they had come from a long distance, it sounded good.

Now I was in a real predicament. It was mid-September and the big smallmouth bite was on, with the perfect weather conditions I knew we could load up on big smallmouth. However, the last thing I wanted was to see a cooler full of 18-20 inch smallmouth. Do I take them to a Class "B" or even a Class "C" spot where they will catch only a few fish, knowing full well that I'll probably never see these guys again, or, do we go to the Class "A" spot, catch a bunch of fish and hope that they become regular clients for many years to come? Well, against my better judgment, I opted to take them to a Class "A" spot only to discover that, once again, I had shot myself in the foot.

Since I knew that they wanted to keep smallmouth I did have to lay down the law. I told them that I didn't want to put any smallmouth over 16 inches in the live well and that they could keep enough for a meal but not a limit. Since they knew that they did not have any choice in the matter they were okay with that, but I figured if they kept some 14-16 inch smallmouth and released some big ones I could demonstrate the importance of maintaining the quality fishery that is present in the river.

The secret spot for the day was one of those spots that cannot be camouflaged. Fishing it is quite simple. You launch the boat, start up the outboard, go about fifty yards and start fishing. Even a complete idiot can figure this one out, but for a guide it is a no brainer. I catch lots of fish in this spot each year. I was hoping that we could catch a few straggler walleyes and a few northern pike so that I could convince Oscar to release the smallmouth. Unfortunately, that was not to be in the cards that day.

Once I positioned the boat on the edge of the weeds near a deep hole I rigged my clients up with red tail chubs. I told Oscar to cast on the right side of the boat and his partner to cast on the left side of the boat. Just as I was starting to explain the type of cover we were fishing, Oscar yelled, "Got One!" Well, Oscar was right and within a few seconds a 20 inch smallmouth went flying out of the water. As far as I was concerned it was a good thing the smallmouth jumped since it threw the hook. After the smallmouth threw the hook, Oscar yelled, "That was the biggest smallmouth I have ever seen."

Before Oscar could make another cast, his partner had a fish and this one didn't get away. After a bit of negotiation the guy stuffed a 17 inch smallmouth into the livewell. The smaller 17 inch smallmouth was caught on the deeper side of the boat which was closer to the shoreline. His buddy made a few more casts and caught another smallmouth that went into the livewell while Oscar did not connect with another 20 incher.

I managed to convince them that to catch more smallmouth we had to move over to the deeper water where Oscar's partner had been catching his fish. I did not tell them that if we moved a bit shallower and fished into the weeds that we would find all the big fish. Now if they would have been conservation minded anglers we could have caught many a five pound smallmouth that day. Since they were cooler fisherman I would try to avoid catching too many big fish that day.

Actually, they were quite content catching the 16 to 17 inch smallmouth since they were bigger than anything they had seen back down in Arkansas. We stayed in that spot all day since I did not want to make a move and show them any more fish holding areas. We ended up putting more smallmouth in the livewell than I had intended but the action was good that day and I think one of them would slip in a fish when I was netting a fish for the other.

Fishing For Smallmouth Bass

They paid me, took their fish, and went on their way leaving me quite unsure what to think of the situation. My clients were happy with the results since they had plenty of fish for supper and had seen the biggest smallmouth of their lives. I knew that they would fish the spot for the next few days so I crossed it off my list for the rest of the week. Besides Oscar and his partner, they had two more guys up with them and they also would be fishing the spot. However, being that they were from Arkansas I thought that I would not see them anymore, at least not that year.

About two weeks later I was fishing the spot by the boat landing with a client and we were catching a few nice smallmouth; everything looked great. It was mid-week in late September and fishing pressure is almost nonexistent that time of year. I told my client that the big smallmouth usually hold just off the weeds about 40 feet in front of the boat. Just when everything seemed under control, a black pickup truck towing a small Jon boat pulled into the landing.

Instead of immediately launching their boat which is the norm, four guys got out of the truck and stood there examining the landing and looking at me and my client. It took a while but they eventually launched the Jon boat and loaded it up with gear. Two guys jumped into the Jon boat and with a rear mount electric trolling motor they inched towards me. Two other guys with lawn chairs, arms full of tackle and a minnow bucket walked the shoreline.

It did not take long for me to feel like General Custer at the Little Big Horn. In front of me within casting distance was Oscar and his son, while from the shoreline I had chubs flying at me with bobbers. I was surrounded with no place to go. Making matters worse, Oscar tied into a gigantic smallmouth, the one that I had been trying to catch for my client that was holding in the weeds in front of the boat. A few minutes later the guys fishing from shore tied into what looked like an 18-19 incher. Oscar did release his giant smallmouth but his buddy fishing from shore put his on a stringer. I knew these guys weren't going anywhere so I told my client we needed to make a move.

Despite our interruption, we caught many nice smallmouth that day but I could not get Oscar and his bunch off my mind. My client and I discussed the matter several times throughout the day and all it did was tick us off more. It is one thing to return to the spot after fishing with a guide but it is more than a bit rude and intrusive when you surround the guide and start taking pot shots at him.

I know that they made one more trip up to the Northwoods for a few meals of tasty smallmouth fillets. Hopefully, they will not return next year but if they do, hopefully my worst case scenario won't come true and they'll decide against chartering a bus, camping out at the boat landing and have themselves a bank fishing tournament and fish fry! So much for the Secret Spots....

Even with the implementation of catch and release, there are many more anglers who hoard their catches. Over the years I have seen many violations, and while the percentage of violators has shrunk among anglers, those that do violate take more than their fair share. What really ticks me off even more than the actual act of violating is how people like the aforementioned old timer justify their defiance of the law.

Unfortunately, there are still plenty of disgruntled old coots who have a defiant attitude toward today's fishing regulations. This past year, I was fishing a reservoir on the Menominee River with a man and his wife during the catch and release bass season. We were having a great time and I was enjoying watching the man cast a chartreuse popper with his fly rod. The smallmouth had just completed spawning and they were gently sucking in the popper and if he was not alert, he would miss the strike. His wife was also catching her share of smallmouth on my old reliable surface bait, the Hubs Chub.

We covered lots of water and although we found ourselves alone on the reservoir, we noticed one old guy fishing from shore. We didn't pay much attention to him until I noticed him fill an orange pail with water. I told my clients that he must be perch fishing since he was using bobbers. I saluted his choice of spots, commenting that besides perch it is a good spot for northern pike and smallmouth bass. Since he was in the spot, I decided to move, thinking that I would return to that spot later in the day.

It continued to be a good day but we had not caught any big smallmouth. The entire day every smallmouth we caught turned out to be a male that had left the beds and was cruising the shorelines or holding tight to wood. I knew that even if we did not catch any more smallmouth that we had already had a good day on the water. However, I also knew that one big smallmouth would have made a good day a great day. I knew that if we returned to the area where we saw the bucket fishermen, we would have a good chance of finding a big smallmouth.

I dropped the trolling motor with the bucket fishermen well off in the distance. Gradually I moved towards him but we could not connect with any smallmouth. Finally we were about fifty feet away from him when my client made a perfect cast. His chartreuse popper landed right under a spruce tree. As soon as the popper hit the water a huge smallmouth moved under it and studied the situation but it did not commit. My client made a few more casts, but he could not raise the smallmouth. His wife even made a cast with my famous Wacky Worm but the big smallmouth had crawled back into her hole. I told my clients that the only thing that might trigger that big bass to strike would be a leech or nightcrawler and we had none of the above on board.

The bucket fishermen was watching and as we got closer we could see the big smile on his face. Before I could say anything he hoisted a behemoth smallmouth out of his pail for all the world to see. I yelled, "You know that it is illegal to have a smallmouth bass in your possession?"

He yelled back, "It ain't illegal if you don't get caught," and he dropped the big bass back into his pail. I commented to my clients that I wondered how many other big smallmouth
were in that pail.

Making matters worse, as we moved down the shoreline, we watched as the bucket fishermen made a long cast towards the spruce tree where we had seen the big smallmouth. About that time I decided to move to another spot, because the last thing I wanted to see was that bobber go down and a big bass engulf the guy's nightcrawler.

Not only had this guy broken the law, but he was basically bragging about it. I am sure he makes a habit of fishing from this spot when the bass are spawning and the season is not open. I only hope that one day the Game warden can catch him in the act of possessing an illegal bass.

It still amazes me how these people have such a blatant disrespect for the law and feel that they are entitled to bending the rules. I guess it is consistent with the entitlement mentality that has become part of American Culture. After all, if you catch the fish of a lifetime by golly, you have the right to keep it.

This past year I had the displeasure of encountering a couple in their fancy custom built canoe over on High Falls Flowage. I was fishing a rock outcropping with two clients when I spotted a couple sliding past us in a hand crafted canoe pushed by an electric trolling motor. At first I paid them no mind until I noticed that they were heading for a rock pile. The rock pile is a great fishing spot and I was planning to make the rock pile my next stop. I told my clients to reel in and that we were going to make a move.

I had plenty of time but I knew I had to reach the rock pile before the canoe. After all, that was my rock pile since I had been fishing High Falls Flowage for over 30 years and I was entitled to the big smallmouth that I just knew was lying in the rocks. All I had to do is start up the outboard and hit the throttle and I could be at the rock pile in no more than 60 seconds. If I swamped the canoe that was their problem, not mine.

Being that I am a nice guy, I moved towards the rock pile at a fast idle and easily overtook the canoe. I had plenty of time to stake my claim on the rock pile and by the time the canoe arrived my client was posing for a photo of himself with a 19 inch smallmouth. The couple in the canoe looked with amazement as we released the smallmouth back into the dark stained water.

The guy in the canoe asked what bait we had caught the smallmouth on and I told him a Case Magic Stick, since I figured he would not have any of them in his canoe. Once they got about 40 feet past my boat, they tossed out an anchor and began untangling their fishing rods. I sat there thinking that we were lucky that the rock pile produced one nice fish before the circus rolled into town.

I continued to circle the rock pile with my electric trolling motor and my client caught a 16 inch smallmouth where the rocks dropped to 25 feet of water. Since we caught another fish I decided to give the rock pile one more pass. By the time we got to the back side of the rock pile, the couple in the canoe had finally started to fish. The guy got his crankbait snagged in the weeds and the woman got her nightcrawler snagged in the rocks. Things did not look good for the anglers in the canoe, but we were enjoying the entertainment.

Just as my client was commenting about their lack of fishing expertise the guy yelled that he had a fish on. The fish hit either a nightcrawler or leech that he had setting on the bottom. We watched as a 20 inch smallmouth broke water and all the while the woman was yelling that she could not find the net. Now, that is pretty bad when your small canoe is so heavily loaded that you can't find the net. Finally, the woman located the net and she scooped the big smallmouth out of the water, pitching it atop the pile of junk in the canoe.

I could hear the guy tell the woman that that was the largest smallmouth he had ever caught and he was going to mount it. We could see the smallmouth jumping around in the canoe and I was hoping that it would bounce its way back into the water. He eventually was able to grab the smallmouth but it released itself, not into the water but back into the canoe before the woman could snap a picture. It took a while but eventually the woman did take a few pictures.

Next, we watched as the guy placed the smallmouth on a stringer and

Fishing For Smallmouth Bass

tossed it in the water. Before I could give my opinion on the matter, one of my clients let the couple know that the harvest of smallmouth bass was illegal at this time of year.

The guy quickly replied, "Oh Yeah! I forgot that we are fishing north of Highway 64. But this is the largest bass I have ever caught and I should be able to keep it to put it on the wall"

We could not believe what we heard and it was evident that he was not going to release the big smallmouth. I whispered to my clients that it was the Friday before the Memorial Day Weekend and hopefully these people would have a rendezvous with a Game Warden. Somehow I don't think that the Game Warden would agree that just because it was the largest bass this man had ever caught he should be entitled to keep it.

Another old timer that thought he had it all figured out was the guy who had multiple stringers hanging over the side of his boat. This guy would anchor in the Menominee River, set up three rods rigged with nightcrawlers and sit in the same spot for hours. Eventually, smallmouth would move into the area and I watched while every fish he caught went on one of those stringers dangling over the side of his boat. I don't think he knew how to release a fish. He kept everything he caught!

This guy had an old beat up 14 foot aluminum boat and since he did not have a livewell, the smallmouth went on a stringer. It looked like he was using the stringers to sort out the fish according to their size. The only thing I could figure out was that he was keeping a legal limit on one stringer and if he was confronted by a Game Warden he would release the other stringers into the river. I would guess that each time he was on the water he took home a minimum of 10 to 12 healthy smallmouth.

Made in the USA
Charleston, SC
08 January 2015